LIFE IS
AN
ELEVATOR

Dedication

To those who 'for your own good'
unwittingly set us on the
downward journey –
We Understand and Forgive you.

To those we hurt when we were
at the bottom –
We ask your Forgiveness.

To those who helped us on the way up –
We thank you.

The Maisner Centre for Eating Disorders is at:

P.O. Box 464,
Hove,
East Sussex.
BN3 2BN
Telephone: Brighton (0273) 729818/29334

Paulette Maisner now has consulting rooms in the City of London
and South West London. There are also many branches of The Maisner Centre
throughout the country.
Details of your local branch, postal courses and consultations are
available by sending a large stamped addressed envelope to the above address.

Compulsions is the only magazine dedicated exclusively to failed dieters,
compulsive eaters, bulimics, anorexics, their families and their friends. This bi-
monthly magazine is available by mail order only and will be sent in a plain
wrapper. For a sample copy, send £1.65 (cheque or postal order) payable to
Maisner Publishing Limited, to Maisner Publishing Limited, Dept. L.E., Linton
House, Linton Road, Loose, Maidstone, Kent, ME15 0AD.

LIFE IS

▲N

ELE▼ATOR

HOW TO OVERCOME COMPULSIVE BEHAVIOUR
AND THE UPS AND DOWNS OF LIFE

PAULETTE MAISNER
AND ROSEMARY TURNER

Lennard Publishing
1989

Lennard Publishing

a division of Lennard Books Ltd.

Musterlin House,
Jordan Hill Road,
Oxford,
OX2 8DP

British Library Cataloguing in Publication Data

Maisner, Paulette
Life is an Elevator
1. Man. Appetite disorders. Therapy
I. Title
616.85'2
ISBN 1 85291 042 9

First published 1989
© Paulette Maisner and Rosemary Turner 1989

Design by Forest Publication Services, Luton, Beds.
Typeset by Origination, Dunstable, Beds.
Cover design by Pocknell and Co.
Reproduced, printed and bound in Great Britain by
Butler and Tanner Limited, Frome.

The authors wish to thank all those who helped with this project and who gave their
permission to reproduce material within it. If they have inadvertently omitted to
contact anyone whose assistance has enhanced this book, they would like to hear
from them.

CONTENTS

PROLOGUE

'I don't want to talk about me; what about *you*?'

Inevitably this is the first thing clients ask me when they come to the Maisner Centre for Eating Disorders for help. They aren't ready to open up to me at this early stage; they want to know what *I've* been through first – to find out why they should put their confidence in me.

And as I tell my story, I see recognition grow on their faces as they realise they are listening to a fellow sufferer. There is relief there too: 'But that's just what happened to me!' and 'You've done that too?!'.

As I am speaking, they begin to feel that I will understand their problems – because I have been there myself.

This book gives the story I have told to so many of my clients – my credentials, as it were, for being able to help them. My self-help guide is not based on dry theory gleaned from learned textbooks; it is based on my own experience. It is the method I devised and used myself as I slowly climbed out of the mess my life was in, and up the staircase to the penthouse.

PART 1

WHEN THE PENNY DROPS

As the train pulled out of Victoria Station I began settling myself down in my usual restless way for the journey home to Brighton. I got up to put my briefcase on the rack, sat back in the corner seat, then reached across to get a cigarette from my bag. I rummaged around for the magazine I had bought to read on the journey but it lay open on my lap as I gazed at the world slipping by, too shattered to make much sense of what I was reading.

It had been one of those frantic and frustrating Mondays, from the early morning dash for a packed commuter train to this late rush back across London for the trip home. One of those mixed days of stimulation and frustration that lifts you to an exhilarating high, then knocks you down to an irritating low, leaving you finally in a state of wrung-out exhaustion, but knowing you will be back for more next week.

As principal of the Maisner Centre for Eating Disorders my work is to see people who suffer from compulsive eating problems and to introduce them to my method of getting their eating back under control. Although each case is individual the course is flexible enough to help each one. First of all there is a consultation, the chance to talk about something which is usually kept a closely guarded secret. Then each client is sent away to fill in food charts. They have to write down everything they eat as well as when, where and in what mood they ate, so I can begin to analyse when eating binges occur and grasp what is the real root of the problem. They are given a sensible eating plan to follow, and must keep in regular contact with the Centre to monitor progress. My clients are not people who just love food and over-indulge; their eating is closely linked to their emotional state and we work on sorting out the underlying personal problems so that food and bingeing are no longer important. It is hard and demanding work, but very necessary: the thousands of files of clients past and present that fill my office prove what a widespread problem this is.

When I was offered the chance to work at a prestigious London hospital and a health centre in the City for one day a week in addition to the Maisner Centre's head office in Brighton, I jumped at the opportunity. I realised right from the start it would be anything but easy for me – I was the person who just a few years ago would have been incapable of even travelling by tube. But I knew it was an important career step to take because not only would it expand my field of work, but it meant that the Maisner Centre for Eating Disorders was being recognised by professional people as a genuine and worthwhile means of tackling the huge and largely misunderstood problems of compulsive eating.

After a lifetime struggling with my own eating problems I know I am well-qualified to call myself an expert on the subject. I have no medical training; but my diplomas in the school of life rank more than equal to the college certificates that usually hang on consulting room walls. And how gratifying it is to discover that top doctors and psychologists now understand that compulsive eaters need to be able to relate to the person who is setting out to help them.

The Maisner Centre sees hundreds of people each year, each individual locked in his or her own personal misery of an addiction to food. The help and advice I give them is no wonder cure, no gimmick or trick to mask the dreadful thing that is ruining their life, it is all about recognising problems and planning a new attitude to life that will bring about permanent changes for the better. And it works. I can confidently tell my clients that if they stick with the course they will learn how to get their eating, and their lives, under control. But it is mainly up to them. The genuine desire to make changes and carry them through must come from the individual; I can only advise and support, point out the road they must travel, and tell them it is their choice whether they go that way or not.

Part of the course involves practical advice such as having regular, well-balanced meals, avoiding the severe hunger that precipitates a binge, and keeping blood sugar levels in balance. But other things are just as important, such as learning to improve self-assertion and to cope with stress, and making real changes in lifestyle. When I first started the Maisner Centre I used to believe it was not possible to cure compulsive eating, that the best that could be achieved was to get eating under control. But over the years I have seen so many people become completely and permanently well that my ideas have matured and developed. I can now tell people they can be cured. Many are, but it is a more subtle result than just taking away the urge to binge. The miracle only occurs when the individual has made the changes – sometimes small, sometimes drastic – which were necessary. They then realise that eating is no longer so important, it no longer dominates and overwhelms their life but has shrunk back to realistic proportions. They can put on 2lb and it is not the end of the world, because they have discovered there is more to life than this obsession.

Some people can put their eating addiction behind them for ever, and it becomes a chapter of their life that is now closed. For others, and I myself am one of these, the reaction is still there; at moments of crisis, somewhere ideas turn to food, but it becomes a natural reaction to reason it all out and find alternatives.

That Monday evening, as the train picked up speed across the Thames and headed south, I assessed how I felt and recognised that ten years ago I would not have survived the tough bits of the day to be able to savour the exhilarating times. The stress and pressures would have left me bingeing and boozing all evening, or getting through with the prop of a handful of pills. Nowadays I have learnt to adapt myself to cope with the pressure: I can now begin to appreciate that I really have got my life under control at last, and how worthwhile it is.

As the houses of South London rattled by I wondered how many of those curtained windows masked some huge personal crisis, some life-shattering problem which to me flashing by was no more than a square of lamplight in a dark night. And to them my whole life, my struggles and disasters, were as insignificant as the train racing by their kitchen window.

For a moment I seemed to step outside myself and see just an ordinary woman sitting in a second class carriage – nothing to rouse much interest in a casual observer. It amused me to imagine how surprised the other occupants of the carriage would be if they knew what was going through the mind of the passenger in the corner seat. Beneath the outwardly calm and smart exterior was that same woman who had attempted suicide and caused mayhem one hot summer's night in a Spanish police cell. That must have been 20 years ago – maybe 25 – time loses its meaning when you spend so many years wallowing from day to day in a fog of existence. It stays in my mind as one of the lowest spots of a life that has had no shortage of 'downs'.

But I am the same woman. After a lifetime of choosing a miserable form of escapism, the penny finally dropped for me, and I began the long struggle up to the penthouse.

You don't have to look far to find examples of people who are choosing the route of escapism that I followed for so long. Only the other day I was invited to the opera, and was waiting for my friend and getting some air outside the theatre before it began. As I sat perched on a low wall I saw two familiar figures weaving towards me: Paul and Kim, whom I had encountered at sessions of a local drug and alcohol abuse centre.

They are both in their 20s, and addicted to hard drugs. Paul is also an alcoholic. They spend their days drifting aimlessly around and their nights sleeping under the pier in their ragged, filthy clothes, surviving from one fix to the next. They spotted me and ambled up to ask for money for food, which I handed over. Kim threw her arms round me and kissed me, just as my friend appeared along the street, alarmed to see me in such degenerate company and fearful for my health and safety.

As is usually the case, with Paul and Kim there is a painful story behind the miserable state in which they now exist. Kim was a bright young student who went to a party to celebrate the end of her university final exams. She had a brilliant future ahead of her, but that night she fell down the stairs. She was taken to hospital in terrible pain. The repeated doses of painkillers prescribed to get her through the ordeal set her on the road to drug addiction. Paul, who had been with her and was desperate with guilt over the accident, began drinking, and they slowly slid downhill together.

In a recent newspaper article, I read that the famous film star, Elizabeth Taylor, has once again succumbed to her alcohol addiction, and is also taking 20 tablets a day to deaden her chronic back pain, caused by a riding accident while shooting a film some 40 years ago.

Forces of circumstance, which I tend to call accidents of life, can overwhelm any one of us. Some people are lucky enough to struggle free, others get swept away and find themselves drifting in the scum of life without really knowing how they came to be there. Somewhere they had made the choice to end up there but the reasons were never clear or logical, or even conscious.

Time and again I have met up with people who, like Kim, began their involvement with hard drugs after some health problem for which drugs were freely prescribed by their doctor. When a girl is in terrible pain and a release is offered, who would stop to think she might at that moment be choosing to become a drug addict? As with so many choices it would take superhuman awareness to recognise and appreciate the true nature of a choice when it is offered.

So many people, just like Kim, step into the elevator and start travelling down through one of these accidents of life. Some choose to get back on their own, others are shot back by yet another of life's 'accidents'. Others just keep going on down and down to the basement and never find the way back up. Once on the way down you may occasionally catch glimpses of the outside world, but it seems so far away and so unobtainable, a world inhabited by other people, and the steel door of your cage stands firmly in the way. In my case I readily admit it was psychological reasons rather than some blow of fate that started me on the way down.

There seems to be no pattern to determine who will succeed in keeping life under control and who will be knocked sideways by life's experiences. Money, education, intelligence don't seem to make any difference. One of my most memorable clients is a woman from a wealthy family with all the right social connections who has built up a good career as a surgeon. To the outside world she fits the picture of privilege and achievement, but in fact she is a complete mess. Totally dominated by her mother all her life, the doctor who holds life and death in her hands jumps at her mother's every word. She escapes her intolerable emotional situation through sex, but only when she is drunk enough to fall into bed with any man who comes along. Years of turning to drink have created a new problem which now obliterates the original problem. Drinking has replaced her inability to cope with her mother as the big problem in her life.

I meet ballet dancers who have grown too tall, housewives whose husbands had walked out on them, career people who have been made redundant. They lose sight of the way forward and often it takes an outsider to show them that life does not end at that point unless they choose for it to do so. Other people, however, can only point the way, it is the individual who has to actually make the choice.

Perhaps a good illustration of this is the story of Paul and Charlie, two clients of the Maisner Centre, two young men with compulsive eating problems. Paul's eating problems started when he lost his job and shortly afterwards began to develop hearing problems and became deaf. Now he stays at home all day watching television and thinking about food. He feels he belongs neither in the world of the deaf nor in the world of the hearing, and he has no real ambition to find another job or improve his life in any way. He has chosen a lifestyle that allows him to hide away from his problems but which makes every moment utterly miserable, with no hobbies apart from eating, and a whole range of excuses for not taking an interest in anything. He takes no exercise because he feels so unfit, but he is afraid of putting on weight so he doesn't eat, thus he is growing weaker and less fit from malnourishment. He seems to live on cottage cheese, apples, and endless bars of chocolate in a downward spiral of starving and bingeing, loneliness and misery.

Charlie, at the age of 22, has been in prison since he was 16 and has no idea how long he is going to be confined. Much of his sentence has been spent in solitary confinement and he developed eating problems, but not for long. He chose to take full advantage of every opportunity for education and self-development that prison life could offer him. Most prisoners say it is not worth taking courses because they will only end up unemployed and back inside after their release. But Charlie recognised his unique opportunity to fill in the huge gaps created by limited education and a deprived childhood, which were two important elements in his original involvement in crime.

Charlie avidly reads daily newspapers and a range of magazines to keep in touch with what is going on in the outside world. He fills every moments of his day with painting, a social psychology course, running, weight training, meditation, and generally improving himself. He did a course with me and succeeded in controlling his eating and it only took him a few weeks to get his eating under control. After that he became a penfriend to other compulsive eaters in the outside world and has been a great source of help and support to them.

Although Charlie is a prisoner, he has found the key that unlocks the prison of his own mind; from a very difficult position he has built a positive and fulfilling life for himself. Meanwhile Paul, who has the whole world open to him, remains locked and chained within the constrictions he has built up by his attitude to life.

In many ways the two young men have a lot in common: both have been the victims of accidents of life in different ways; both get pay-offs from the choice of attitude they have adopted. Of course it is in Charlie's interests to be a model prisoner and prove he is worthy of an early release, but although that influenced his early choices, in time the sense of self-fulfilment he got from his busy life made it easier to carry on making positive choices. Paul also has sound reasons for choosing the attitude he lives by. His well-to-do parents give him a comfortable home and his mother is at his beck and call, he does not have to go out into the world and fight to survive, he can make his deafness an adequate excuse for taking the easy way out.

Life is not easy for either young man; Paul feels an outsider among lads of his own age, Charlie is considered a freak by his fellow prisoners and often has to be separated from them for his own safety. But the choices they make now will almost certainly influence the sort of life they will choose for themselves in years to come. Paul's parents will not be around for ever to protect him from the harsh realities of life. He has little self-reliance to fall back on in the future and the years ahead look grim and bleak unless he chooses to make changes. Charlie, however, has the chance of making a good life for himself if he continues to choose to do so. Whatever happens in the future he has at least proved to himself that he can cope and is thus creating the potential for happiness and fulfilment in later years.

Most people with an eating problem who have struggled along for years and not got to grips with it will, if they are honest, probably identify with Paul. When things get tough they choose what they see as the easy way out rather than struggle on for the distant but far greater benefits which are the reward for really getting on top of the problem. Charlie realised comparatively early the greater benefits of choosing to face up to the realities of his life and personality. Perhaps Paul will be one of those for whom it takes longer for the penny to drop; alternatively he may never choose to make changes. It probably all depends on just how bad and uncomfortable his lifestyle becomes. For everyone who decides to make radical changes, there comes a point sooner or later when they just feel they are not prepared to go on in the same old ways a moment longer.

All day long people are telling me about the things they are going to do, the changes they are going to make, but nine times out of ten the next time I see them they are still going on in the same old ways. You get into a rut and it is easy just to carry on as before. Then, after a long time of just talking about it, one day you actually go out and do it and the whole course of your life changes. Why do you choose that day—who can tell?

One client of mine telephoned me at one in the morning saying she had decided to leave her husband. From her case history I knew that there had been serious problems in the marriage for more than 15 years, and even the marriage guidance counsellor had advised them to separate. But this woman was stuck in her rut of eating problems and a bad marriage, and was unable to shift until suddenly she reached the crucial point when she realised she was not going to take any more. In my experience, when the choice is finally made in cases like this, the person will usually stick with it.

The more I see of people and their problems the more convinced I become that we all have a choice about how we live our lives. I can see now that I made choices throughout my life, I chose whether to climb up a floor or ride down a floor in my elevator, even though sadly I may not have been really aware of what I was choosing at the time. I have a picture in my mind of life being like a game of Snakes and Ladders. Just when you think you are doing nicely, some disaster strikes and pushes you right back down again. You feel you are doomed never to progress. But, equally suddenly, some person or event can give you a real boost and you are off and on the way up again. You can choose the rules by which you play: rolling the dice, just playing by chance, is for people who are floundering around not in control of their life, others impose rigid rules of play which limit life to what can be easily coped with. For example, if you were to play Snakes and Ladders by just moving on the even numbered squares you would avoid quite a few snakes, but also a lot of the ladders; life would in some ways be easier, but in others far less fulfilling.

The best way to play the game of life is to deliberately choose the squares you land on and the moves you make, taking responsibility for the consequences. In a game, when you can view the board as a whole, it is easy to make the right decisions each time and always win; perhaps if I could view my life that clearly I would also make the right choices each time.

One of the most difficult things about making choices in life is actually realising there is a choice to be made, and what that choice is. I find that people who have led a fairly normal life until comparatively recently have a better grasp of what alternatives are available to them. They say they want to be like they were five years ago, and that gives them some sort of goal to work to. One of my problems has always been that I don't remember ever being what the world might call a 'normal' person. I've had eating problems since I was six years old and so by the time I was an adult I was not aware that I had the choice to be anything else, or that my eating habits could be different. Deciding to get my eating under control was not like choosing between two dresses in a shop – which one I liked best. It was more like trying to visualise some kind of lovely garment I had never seen when I had worn a dull uniform all my life: the choice was just that much more difficult.

I still have not fathomed out what it was that made me choose to make changes in the end. It happened during the time I was living with my boyfriend Joe, and there is no doubt that he was a tremendous influence on me, and yet many seeds for change had already been sown and by that time were growing ripe for sprouting.

As I raced towards the end of my 30s I truly believed that I would be dead by the age of 40 if I didn't make some changes. I had returned from many years living in Spain to a dingy bedsit in London and found myself surrounded by people even worse than myself. There was an incredible amount of talent hovering around the house in which I rented a room, there were artists, musicians and poets on every floor, and yet nobody had a regular job. I could not ignore the waste of life that was going on all around me.

I used to spend long evenings talking to a man named Jim who was a great philosopher in his way. He said he had never achieved what he wanted to achieve, and he made me see that everyone in that house had a choice to change or end up as bitterly frustrated as he was. He looked fit and healthy to me, but he knew he was riddled with cancer and his days were numbered, and one day he dropped down dead in the room next to mine. I was shocked into realising the message he had been passing on to me, that I too was wasting my life. I had reached a point where I felt I did not want to go on in the same old ways and I at last became more aware of what I was doing and the choices I was making, although I still could not see a definite way forward. It was around that time I met Joe.

Recognising the right time to make a choice is as important as recognising the choice to be made. There are those who never do make the choice for positive changes, they just go on and on avoiding the issue, sinking deeper into depression, drink, drugs or their own particular form of hell which will probably end in an untimely death or suicide.

Barry is one particular person who comes to mind in this respect. He has been an alcoholic for most of his life, not for lack of opportunities to change but from an inability to make the choice to pull himself back. At one point he was offered a place at a top rehabilitation clinic which held a real chance for him to be cured of his drink problem. He got as far as packing his bag ready to go. Then he decided it would be too difficult, so he unpacked and went back to the bottle. Now he is dying; he sees dying as easier than life without drink.

Women stay in bad marriages for years and years, making any number of excuses for the beatings, the neglect, the sheer misery that their husbands impose on them. I see so many women with eating disorders who binge as the only escape they know from their misery, even though their bingeing habits only add an extra load of unhappiness and guilt. Controlling the eating problem means facing up to the lifestyle that is leading to bingeing, so choosing to make changes so often seems much harder than putting up with what has become familiar.

That critical moment when the penny drops, when years of mounting troubles suddenly tip the scales to an instant decision for change, is something very personal to each individual. You can go on ranting and lecturing and advising someone for years to no effect, but then the moment comes and one little word will tip the balance. It is all very well people constantly giving advice, but if, like me, you never learnt how to listen to it, much less act upon it, those words of wisdom are quite useless. This inability to apply what is being said is common among alcoholics – they hear but do not listen. There is always the chance that one day a casual remark might get through.

Inevitably whenever we make choices we are influenced by people and events that surround us or haunt us from the past.

Barry's mother had influenced him by supporting his decision not to go to the clinic for a cure, and in a lifetime of choosing to let his mother make his decisions for him this was just one more thoughtless action. Barry's mother supplies him with alcohol 'because it makes him happy'. If he were cured of his addiction she would lose her little boy who depends on her, and so she is making her choice to keep him an addict, and he is choosing to let it be so.

My parents were a huge influence on me, and, I regret, not for the better. I see myself as a little girl who stole food at the age of six because she was not getting any love or attention. Their attitude to me battered down my self-esteem from a very early age, and it is people with low self-esteem who are too easily influenced by other people and events and find it so hard to make their own independent choices.

As time goes on, I can see that perhaps things in my childhood were not always as I thought, but the damage was done when I learnt to respond to people and events according to the lessons of my early years. I have recently learnt more about my father's family history and appreciate that he too was greatly influenced by his parents. My father's Russian Jewish family was strong on tradition. They believed a man's role in life was to provide money for the support of his wife and children, and that was all. I now see that he brought me up according to ideas he had himself learned from his parents. As a child I could only see him constantly putting me down and depriving me of all love and affection, but now I can appreciate that it was his way of trying to improve me; he constantly corrected me for what he believed was my own good.

When I recently held my first grandchild in my arms it was a moment of sheer emotional joy. My father looked at his great grandchild and told me to put her down, as 'babies belong in cots'. At long last (and it seems I had to become a grandmother to see it) I could recognise my father as the victim of his own upbringing just as much as I am a victim of mine.

As a small child I craved affection from my father and was too young to realise that his personality was such that he did not know how to express emotions and love other than by buying me a new dress or sending me to an expensive school. There is little point in struggling and striving to get someone to love you if they just do not have that love to give.

My brother was five years younger than me and from the day he arrived he was my mother's pet. I was already established as the only child of the family, but my mother had never had much time for me, or made any effort to listen to me or give me the kind of attention I needed and craved. I didn't understand what was happening in my life, all I knew was that one day when I was five years old I was sent away to an aunt in Blackpool. It was not a happy stay because I did not get on with my two cousins and I have horrid memories of being given brains on toast and carrots to eat. When I came home there was my brother asleep in his cot and my beloved dog was no longer there. My mother told me he had run away. I didn't believe it and yelled and screamed with anger. Later on that day I discovered his body, stiff and cold in the dustbin, and I was convinced my mother had murdered him deliberately to upset me. That is quite unlikely, the dog had probably died or been run over and my mother had hidden the body so I would not be upset, but because I felt such resentment towards her I immediately cast her in the role of villain. I hated the new baby on sight and in particular I hated the way he was getting all the fuss and attention. I was overwhelmed by blind rage against him and terribly jealous. One day when our mother was out I dragged him from his cot and beat him black and blue. I don't think my parents realised what I had done, they must have assumed he had just fallen from his cot; even in such a crisis they were blind to what was going on in my mind and emotions.

I know my mother had an eating problem and a drink problem, and it is no secret that she was a compulsive gambler. The strain this put on our family was bound to lead to problems, like the time my grandmother gave me a gold bracelet which disappeared. I got thumped for losing it but I later found the pawn ticket – my mother had pawned it for gambling cash. My father's inability to express love and emotion towards me doubled the odds on my developing serious personality problems as I grew up.

My early schooldays influenced me a lot, of course. From the very first day I was dreadfully shy, and later I was fat and had to wear bands on my teeth, which sapped my self-confidence and lowered my self-esteem still further. I was terrified of being asked a question in class because I felt I was hopeless at expressing myself. My father had spared nothing in pointing out and trying to correct my mumbling and poor expression, with the result that I felt quite incapable of answering the teacher properly in front of the rest of the class. The other children used to tease and bully me and I easily slipped into the role of victim. One of the reasons why I got picked on a lot was because I was Jewish–at least I felt that was the reason because it was something that made me different from other girls. Our school was divided into Christian and Jewish, with separate prayers for girls of each side. On Jewish holidays the other Jewish girls stayed away, but my mother always sent me to school as we did not celebrate religious festivals at home. That was when I was really aware of being singled out for teasing – the only Jewish girl in a school full of Christians. After I passed my 11 Plus exam and moved into the higher school I decided to change this and without telling my parents I officially became a Christian. Not that I was particularly interested in spiritual matters, it was just a lot more convenient to be numbered amongst the Christian set. Perhaps that was the first faint inkling I had that I could choose to make changes in my life if I really wanted to. Up until then I had been totally unaware that another way of life could exist for me.

When I was about 12 years old, due to some unusual circumstances the details of which I have long since forgotten,

I was invited to stay the night at a schoolfriend's home. It was a winter's evening when we got back from school and I carried my bag up to her bedroom.

'How do you survive the cold evenings?' I asked, noting with surprise that there was no electric fire in her bedroom. Puzzled, she replied that she sat downstairs with her family in the evenings until it was time for bed. It took me some time to digest this information. At home I was sent to my room from five o'clock each afternoon and had no idea that families sat and talked and spent time together every day. It seems bizarre now that I should have been so ignorant, but at the time my way of life seemed quite normal, as I had never known anything different.

And isn't that the way it is with so many people? We get comfortably ensconsed in our own personal little ruts and don't even realise what is going on outside, what great opportunities are just sitting there waiting to be seized. After life has knocked us down a few times we lose the desire to get up and punch back. Certainly I knew I was unhappy as a child but there was not much fight left in me to improve things. Shouting at my father was as far as I ever went, and that was an activity that got me absolutely nowhere. I just shouted and screamed to get some reaction from him, waiting for him to either put his arms round me and hug me or strike out and hit me, but it never worked.

As there were no grand positive choices for me to make I just made the subtle ones, like being ill to gain attention. I had discovered that when I was unwell I didn't have to go to school, everyone was nice to me and I was given special food to eat. However, those sorts of things were negative choices.

If we could really tune into ourselves clearly we could probably always make the right sort of choices. So many of the people I come across who have made wrong choices in life are those who have been greatly influenced by other, stronger characters, who allowed them to cloud their instinctive better judgement. Imagine for example a woman who became a nun because her mother said she had to. Put like this it sounds ridiculous that she took such a huge step without it really being what she wanted, and spent years allowing bitterness and resentment to poison her life. But the pressures on her from early childhood must have been tremendous, and she never truly realised that in fact she was free to choose to do something else with her life.

I recently discovered a wonderful quotation from Buddha which exactly expresses my own feelings about how important it is not to let other people's influence sway our own better judgements: 'Believe nothing, no matter where you read it or who said it – no matter if I have said it – unless it agrees with your own reason and your own common sense'.

Because I firmly believe in the concept of choice, I also believe many of our problems are of our own making. Through ignorance, fear, or a variety of negative influences, we allow ourselves to make the wrong choices time and again. It is obvious that people have different breaking points, different levels at which they are able to remain coping and in control. I know I was never taught how to cope, in particular how to cope with failure. In my family if you did not succeed you were a failure and the stress of trying to live up to that high ideal made me choose failure time and again throughout my childhood and later life.

When I was young I was an excellent swimmer but when my parents came to watch me try for a swimming medal I got in a total panic and failed dismally. I was also a competent horse rider, yet when they came to watch me in a gymkhana I fell off. For a whole string of reasons I chose to live up to the expectation of failure which I assumed they held. And that attitude became a habit that influenced the choices I made for many years to come.

When I am trying to explain something important to somebody and they don't understand what I am saying I can still feel the old feeling of frustration coming up through my stomach, just as if I was still five years old and stamping my foot and shouting at my father to make him understand. Infants suffer greatly from the frustrations of communicating with adults, but with love and patience they can learn how to express themselves clearly and cope when adults don't understand them. My father just told me not to mumble, being more concerned with correcting my speech than with reaching out to discover what thing of vital importance his small daughter was trying to say. The result was that I became quite a foot stamper but never had my wishes heeded, and I believe that early frustration in communication lay at the root of my eating problems.

When I became a mother myself, although I did not observe all the social conventions of motherhood, and my son did not have the outward trappings of security and respectability which my family associated with a proper childhood, he was certainly not emotionally deprived of love in the way I feel I had been as a child. I remember on one occasion he had done something particularly naughty and I gave him a good beating because in the passion of the moment I responded in the only way I knew to get through to him that he had done wrong. Like anyone in the grip of eating problems I suffered from mood swings, and the rage and frustration of bingeing could make me do things I would not normally have done. Because I loved Peter more than anything in the world I soon made it up to him with loving and cuddles, but later I punished myself through bingeing as a reaction to the guilt I felt for hitting him in my frustration and anger.

I still have a scar on my finger where my mother in a blind rage lashed out at me with a carving knife while she was chopping food in the kitchen one day. I told everyone she had tried to cut my finger off, but now I recognise that it was probably the emotional trauma of her own eating problems that made her act in such an uncontrolled way. Perhaps people investigating abuse of children should look more closely at the eating habits of the parents.

Like so many girls I was taught that 'nice girls' don't get angry, and I know I am very far from being alone as a victim of that particular taboo. The drug abuse centres and alcoholic clinics are full of people who learnt this lesson years ago and forgot how to express their overpowering emotions in an appropriate manner.

'Nice girls don't ...' is responsible for a lot of misery in the world. We like to think our society is a lot more free and easy since the Swinging Sixties, today's youngsters are more likely to be allowed to do and say as they please than those born over 40 years ago. But in its own way each generation continues to pile guilt and restrictions on to the next. Children learn from parents and family circumstances how to behave and how to react to the world, and if the parents have too rigid a view of life they will impose their ideas on their children whether it suits the child's nature or not. Strict discipline is particularly found in families where it is part of the father's profession, such as the army or police, and parents who believe they have a certain social position to maintain can also impose rigid rules of behaviour on their children. In fact strict behaviour patterns can be found in every stratum of society: it may be a religious tradition or a cultural one, or purely a prejudiced view of society that demands that children in a family follow the beliefs and lifestyle of the parents without consideration of individual personality.

In my household the image of the 'nice Jewish girl' was constantly held up as an example, an example I constantly failed to live up to. In such families some children turn out carbon copies of their parents and seem to thrive on the security of the restrictions imposed on them. Other children, if they have the self-esteem to stand up for themselves, will openly rebel against what their family try to impose on them, but if, like me, the child wants to rebel but does not know how to begin, the fight is turned inwards and is expressed in other ways, such as some form of anti-social or compulsive behaviour.

When I was a child our family must have appeared quite normal and respectable to the casual observer. Mother and father, son and daughter, living in a spacious flat with the right address, the father successfully providing for his family through his business, the children privately educated, well-dressed, well-mannered. But behind the scenes things were very different. My father's whole life revolved around his work and supplying the right material things of life, and as far as I can remember my mother was always too wrapped up in her own emotional problems to know what was going on around her. My brother was away at boarding school for long periods of time, and I was just an isolated, unhappy and totally helpless little girl. I knew instinctively there was something very wrong with our family and it made me unhappy, although I had no way of understanding it all. It must have appeared that as a child I had everything I wanted, but in fact I felt starved of all things I truly desired.

I felt nobody cared about me, and I longed to be loved. Throughout my childhood I desperately wanted love and attention from my parents but it always seemed to escape me. I had many things that other girls would have sacrificed much for – nice clothes, a room of my own, records and books, and plenty of time to myself. How happily I would have sacrificed my new dresses, my riding lessons, my long evenings alone with a book, for the happy companionship of a loving family life!

So deep was my craving for attention that when, at the age of 14, I was raped, I found there was something about the experience I actually enjoyed. Although the rape itself was pretty messy, the realisation that when that man put his arms round me he wanted me rather than anyone else made it special. I was on holiday with my parents at the seaside and had been taking diving lessons, but just as I was beginning to get quite good at it my father stopped the lessons saying all that springing was bad for my feet. I was bitterly disappointed: once again something I wanted had been dangled in front of me and then snatched away. Angry and hurt, I wandered down to the beach late that evening when it was dark. A man (it may only have been a boy, I don't remember any details about him) began following me and started to talk to me. I talked back and in the dark he caught hold of me and pulled me down on the sand. I never told my parents or anyone else what had happened; although I was shaken, at the same time I was happy that someone in the world actually wanted me. I was prepared to be the victim because I saw myself as 'fat and horrible' and not worth anything better.

Because I was fat, my mother tried to bribe me into losing weight by offering me £1 for every pound of fat I lost. I was taken to a Harley Street doctor who prescribed amphetamines to help me slim. I was 12 years old. Amphetamines, commonly known as speed, keep you awake and suppress the appetite. They are no longer prescribed and are illegal to buy these days, but 40 years ago few people acknowledged their addictive qualities. My downward path into addiction to speed began in the consulting room of that Harley Street specialist, and I can see how other familiar thought patterns were being formed at that time which were to grow into monsters that took over my last shreds of common sense: food instead of love, money and gifts instead of attention, a comfortable house to live in but no loving home, drugs to make my body conform instead of careful counselling to sort out my troubled mind. By the time I reached physical maturity food, drink and drugs were already a way of life to me, but many years went by before I reached any kind of maturity of mind and emotions where I could see these things for what they were – habitual props against the harshness of reality.

We can earnestly ask to be loved and cared for, yet if time and again we choose a partner who does not have that sort of love to give we end up lonely and unhappy. Which brings me back to the Maisner Centre and the hundreds of stories people tell me of their life histories. All those lips saying, 'I want to get my eating under control', all those pens writing, 'I want to change my life', and all those individuals choosing to carry on bingeing and vomiting and being miserable because they are not prepared to make the changes that are essential. Those people do not achieve what they say they want; they are stuck with the consequences of what they have chosen to do.

On a Monday night when I get home tired, irritable, worn out, I know I can choose to have a few drinks, or perhaps a good old binge. Or I can choose to have a relaxing bath, water my plants and go off to bed satisfied with the achievements of the day. I know I have the choice, and I know which choice I shall be making.

WIFE, MOTHER AND DRIFTER

Last Summer I was invited to a dinner organised by a local charity. A friend had tickets and I had a free evening so we went, not expecting anything earth-shattering to occur. And on the face of it nothing did, except that I came face to face with one of those moments of sudden realisation of just how much I and my life have changed. Big crises and events can affect our lives deeply, but sometimes it is just the little things that prove significant landmarks on the road of change. On that evening it was the ice cream.

It is ten years since I last tasted ice cream. I booted it out along with puddings, sweets and sugar in my coffee when I read up on the importance of stable blood sugar levels to physical and emotional health. Anyone with a sweet tooth knows how difficult it is to battle with the cravings for sugar, the longing for that quick energy boost (and the inevitable low that follows). I used to adore ice cream in the old days, eating it by the tub, any flavour, but when the time came to make changes ice cream was something that was firmly banned.

On this particular evening there was a set menu and ice cream was served up as dessert. The dish was put in front of me, and all of a sudden I said to myself, 'Why not? Eating is no longer a problem to me, I can handle one dish of ice cream if I want'. I felt a strange rush of excitement as I lifted the spoon to my lips after so many years – but what a disappointment! It tasted awful, far too sweet, and the coldness hurt my teeth. Not only had the battle been won, the war was over. . . I don't like ice cream any more.

As far back as I can remember I would do anything to get my hands on sweets: lie, cheat, steal, the desire for sugary comforts was far stronger than any moral code. During my schooldays sweets were not that easy to come by with the War and rationing, so my most vivid memory of the school in Switzerland I was sent to at the age of 15 is of discovering the joys of chocolate. Nothing else about that expensive education that was supposed to make a well-finished young lady of me gives me much pleasure to recall. The other girls all seemed so full of confidence, as if they had been brought up to believe they were a cut above the rest of the world. I was totally introverted, I just sat in silence most of the time while the other girls teased me without mercy. I didn't make a single friend.

My parents sent me to Switzerland in the hope it would help my sinus problems, and it wasn't long before I discovered that just like at home it was only when I was ill that people were nice to me. A bout of illness was the only thing guaranteed to bring me a bit of attention and sympathy, and it also let me escape from the dreaded skiing lessons which I hated because I was far too fat to cut any kind of figure on the ski slopes.

By the time I left Switzerland I was fatter than ever. Apart from the glorious chocolate which was freely available to girls with money, we used to go to dances on Saturdays and while other girls were dancing, making eyes at the boys and flaunting their expensive clothes, I was knocking back the alcohol. Probably lots of other girls were drinking and getting into trouble as well – I remember a scandal over the daughter of a peer, who got pregnant – but I was so wrapped up in myself I took it for granted that I was the only one who was lonely and thoroughly miserable.

I came home from Switzerland with some sketchy secretarial skills and the ability to speak French. Things were just as bad at home between myself and my parents, so I decided to move out. I got myself a bedsit at Notting Hill Gate while I drifted from job to job – surviving, but only just.

One day I saw an advertisement for girls to demonstrate Marianne Margarine, a new product that was being launched in the West Country. Always looking for a change in my circumstances, I applied and got the job, which involved handing out samples of margarine in the big stores of Devon dressed in Scandinavian costume. After work the Marianne girls were put up in a big hotel for the duration of the promotional tour, and it was there that I met my husband.
I had never really had the opportunity to meet men before. From a secluded childhood, through adolescence at an all-girls' school, boys and men had been something far removed from my limited experience. I suppose, as in most Jewish

families, it had been taken for granted that I would one day marry a solicitor or a dentist and set up a respectable home of my own, but that prospect was as far removed from reality for me as my whole upbringing had been. Dates with boys to dances or the pictures were foreign to me; I had no idea how to hold a conversation with a man, much less form any kind of relationship with one.

My husband was older than me although I doubt if he was emotionally any more mature. There is little doubt that as far as I was concerned his overwhelming attraction was that he seemed to take a real interest in me. Having to date been starved of affection from anyone, to be suddenly the centre of another person's attention for the first time in 17 years completely bowled me over. My life up till then had been a mess, but here was the perfect way out, a chance to escape from the loneliness and insecurity of being single, and an opportunity to show the world that even though I was fat I could easily get a husband. Without telling anyone, not even my parents, we made our wedding plans and, caught up in the spur of a romantic moment, we ran away to Gretna Green and got married.

Our marriage was about as doomed as any could be. I had drifted into it, the way I had drifted through my life to that point, and I must have been an impossible wife because, with my low level of self-esteem and my insecurity, I behaved totally unreasonably. If he was late home from work I would be mad with jealousy, demanding to know where he had been and what he had been doing. When we were out together he never even dared smile at a shop assistant for fear of upsetting me. In my desperate state I demanded his total attention at all times and must have put an unbearable load on him.

We lived with his parents after our wedding, and I felt right from the start that his mother did not like me. It didn't help matters when I became pregnant almost immediately. I don't think my husband was any more ready to become a parent than I was. The constant fights and arguments made me more and more depressed, on top of feeling that his mother thought I was not good enough for her darling little boy. I felt my husband was constantly criticising me, and realised with horror that he seemed to be growing daily more and more like my father.

After just three months of marriage our relationship was already on the rocks. My husband stayed out later and later to avoid me, I was terrified by the idea of having a baby, and the two of us just rowed and fought because he did not want the baby any more than I did. Weeks went by and I became severely depressed, until one day I swallowed an overdose of sleeping tablets, and from then on the rest of my pregnancy was spent in a psychiatric hospital.

In those days suicide was still a criminal offence, and although I was not prosecuted for my attempt to kill myself I was made to feel very guilty. It was made clear to me that I either went into the psychiatric hospital as a voluntary patient until just before the baby was born, or I would be committed. So I agreed to go without any arguments, and once there I suppose I quite enjoyed the experience. I was something of a pet with the nurses because I was expecting a baby, there was nothing seriously wrong with me and I did not receive any medical treatment. The whole arrangement was an easy cop out for everyone, including me.

Even when I was established as a patient my husband did not come to see me; he was no more willing or able to take on the responsibility of having me back at home than I was capable of looking after myself, so it was agreed it was better and safer for everyone if I stayed where I was.

During those months I came the closest I have ever been to anorexia nervosa because I nearly stopped eating for a time. This was of no great concern to anyone as I was so overweight to begin with, but the nurses used to take extra time with me coaxing me to eat and I can't pretend I didn't enjoy the attention. In psychiatric terms I was probably reverting to being a baby myself and not taking responsibility for growing up, but in my mind I felt I was punishing those I felt were responsible for putting me in that place. In a way food was the only thing that I had any control over at that time, the only bit of power I could wield.

Right through my pregnancy I was terrified by the thought of the coming baby, and had made up my mind I would have it adopted immediately. Then a few days before the birth was due, when I was once more out in the world, I went to visit the maternity ward and was shown a new born baby. It was my first experience of a real live baby, apart from jealous rages against my little brother when I was five years old, and the infant went straight to my heart. In a sudden turn-around I knew I wanted my baby more than anything else in the world, and when Peter actually arrived I decided that motherhood was the best thing that had ever happened to me.

In the days after the birth I was put in a ward with five other new mothers. It was the hospital rule that babies were kept in the nursery and only brought out at feeding time, but I flatly refused to be parted from Peter and caused uproar as I demanded he stay by me day and night. In the years that followed, throughout his childhood I could never stay far away from him for long. He remained the best thing that ever happened in my life.

Eventually I went back home to my husband. My parents paid the rent on a flat for us in an endeavour to keep us together, but in no time at all the rows started again. We soon agreed on one thing though – that Peter would be better off with one loving parent than two fighting ones, so I left taking Peter with me, and he has never seen his father again since then. In time my husband and I were divorced and that chapter of my life was closed for good.

In my work at the Maisner Centre I see many examples of women who are not happy with their marriage and develop all sorts of problems, including eating problems, as a result. When I am talking to a client and it sounds as if an unhappy relationship could well be adding to an eating or drinking problem, I often recommend some sort of counselling help such as marriage guidance. I usually meet with a lot of misconceptions about this, such as that it is only for married couples, and that they will tell you to patch up your differences no matter what the circumstances. Marriage guidance is not for settling occasional arguments, it is designed to resolve long-term breakdown in a relationship. Each partner is seen separately by a counsellor, and the couple are seen together in an attempt to work things out for the benefit of everyone. That may mean advising divorce if the breakdown seems irreparable. Apart from the possibilities of getting relationship problems sorted out, I point out to clients that the act of seeking professional help is a positive and beneficial action in itself.

Judy is one of my clients whom I directed towards marriage guidance counselling. Her husband was self-employed and worked long hours so Judy was left at home alone a lot and used to eat to fill the gap. The counsellor suggested a contract between the two partners which required them to go out together two nights a week, and they began to do this, but it didn't solve Judy's problems. They found on their nights out that they had nothing to talk about – each had become locked in their own world. So he drank and she ate as they dutifully fulfilled their contract to each other. Judy had thought her problem was her husband going out so much, but in fact it was more to do with her having no interests and life of her own to fall back on. From eating because he was out she had progressed to actually *wanting* him to go out so she could be alone to binge – a much more insidious state of mind. So the contract was not really giving Judy what she wanted, and it failed. The next step was for her to recognise what the real problem was. She went to an evening class on her own one night a week, began to make a few friends, and then found when she did go out with her husband they had something to talk about, and the relationship improved greatly, as did Judy's eating problems.

So many problems seem to crop up in relationships where people are not communicating. Time and again I see people making huge assumptions about other people and acting on what they assume the other is thinking. My tactic is to challenge the assumption, and it is usually received with bewilderment or disbelief. Often it is so much easier to assume you know what is going on in someone else's mind and apply your own interpretation to what they do and say, rather than being brave enough to find out the truth through discussion and communication.

Let me give you the example of Angela who didn't get on with her mother-in-law. 'My mother-in-law doesn't like me', she used to tell me time and again, and I was reminded of myself at the age of 17 living with my husband's mother and totally unable to get through to her or communicate, just assuming she didn't like me because I was married to her son. One day, in exasperation at hearing yet another of Angela's moans about the in-laws, I asked her straight out how she knew what the woman was thinking: had she ever told her in so many words she disliked her?

'I can see the look in her eye whenever she comes to visit us,' was Angela's reply. It suited her to think her mother-in-law was criticising her, it was an assumption that covered all the reasons why the relationship with the in-laws was strained, and gave her the excuse to be unsociable and difficult with her husband's parents. No actual word of criticism had ever been spoken, but Angela contined to cling to her assumptions and refused to take the first step towards a more understanding relationship.

Just as you should never make assumptions about others, you should never assume that other people know what is going on in your mind. I remember one occasion when I was going out for the evening with a pleasant, well-mannered man. I had hurt my shoulder and was annoyed with him for not offering to help me on with my coat. Being in pain and a bit grumpy, I complained at his bad manners and he said that so many women object to old-fashioned courtesies he never offered them these days. That put me in my place for making assumptions about his manners; once he knew I liked being helped into my coat he always made a point of doing it.

Recently I realised I am still guilty of making wrong assumptions, of jumping to the wrong conclusions. It was during one of my Aerobics in Water classes, and our teacher shouted out down the length of the pool, 'Paulette! Stomach in!

Mortified, I tensed my muscles even more tightly, feeling about 2 foot high–and twice as wide.

It was only when she repeated the command later that I realised she hadn't been singling me out at all. What she actually said was 'Pull that stomach in!'–a general exhortation to us all to stand up straight!

I am no longer surprised at the scale of how many people live through a marriage just making assumptions about what their partner is thinking or wanting, or not wanting. I say to people time and again, that unless they actually ask and get a reply, all their assumptions could be little more than fantasy. Joan was a typical example, a housewife who kept her house clean and well-ordered. When the children grew up she decided to go back to full-time work, but the extra load of running a job and a house began to get on top of her. She seethed inside because her husband never offered to do his share of the housework or even wash up after the evening meal. I got them together one day and asked the husband, in front of her, why he did not help in the house now his wife had a full-time job. He looked surprised and said he had no idea she wanted help, she always seemed to have everything so well under control with her set routines that he had assumed she would be annoyed if he interfered. They were both making assumptions about what the other thought and were not communicating their grievances to each other, but in this case it could all be sorted out so easily.

More often than not, making wrong assumptions is just one more result of low self-esteem. The person who does not respect themselves or see themselves as worthy of being treated better by others is not able to stand up and challenge the behaviour of others. Such a person finds it much easier to make assumptions, and too often those assumptions are unfavourable to themselves; they assume others are thinking badly of them when maybe they are hardly considering them at all. Low self-esteem was the curse of my early life, the root of so many of my problems, and the reason why I married so young and so hastily. I did not respect myself enough to be able to build a worthwhile relationship with my husband or his family, I rushed into marriage thinking it would all be happy ever after and when I found I was even more miserable than before I drifted on to a new page of life, scrubbing out the one with marriage written on it and starting a new sort of scribbled living.

What came along next was that I met a girl who was full of enthusiasm for going to Spain to set up a business, and I got caught up with her plans.

I decided to leave Peter with my mother for a while. I had no intentions of leaving him for long, but it seemed impossible to go off hitchhiking abroad and setting up a new business venture with a small child in tow. I soon discovered I missed him dreadfully and once I was established with a home in Spain I went back to England to collect him.

My mother refused to give him up.

I already knew how much I hated her but this was beyond anything she had ever put me through before. I went to court, and there was a very bitter legal battle of daughter against mother, which I won. Then Peter and I went back to Spain. There was never a shortage of baby minders, the Spanish adore children and Peter was an adorable child, so he was always well cared for and happily amused when I chose to go out on the town.

When my friend and I first arrived in Spain, we were drifting, not making much success of our business plans, until inevitably I met a new man, one who I thought offered me what I was looking for.

I was hitchhiking near Valencia one day when I was caught in one of those torrential Mediterranian cloudbursts. A car stopped and, soaked to the skin and dripping all over the expensive upholstery, I got in but the driver did not seem too concerned as we crawled on through the deluge. The weather got worse and a cascade of rain and mud and boulders came hurtling down the hillside, bringing the car to a halt and stranding us miles from anywhere for 24 hours. During that time we got to know each other fairly well: his name was Evaristo and he was a businessman and mayor of his town. I told him I was hitching around trying to get settled, and by the time our adventure was over and we could drive on to his destination he had offered to rent a flat for me to live in near his home.

I knew he was married with a family and a social position to maintain, but it was quite acceptable for someone in his position to keep a mistress so I was displayed around his social circle and produced as an 'asset' to promote his image. I might have looked like a drowned rat when he first set eyes on me, but I always made sure I looked my best after that whenever I knew he was likely to call. Because I knew he cared about me and took an interest in me I felt more inclined to look after myself and be glamorous for his benefit. I studied Spanish language and literature at twice-weekly classes until my Spanish became fluent. This was when Peter came to live with me; he adored Evaristo.

Evaristo tried to make me happy in his own way when my whole life revolved around him, but it was always very much on his terms and I totally lacked the self-esteem to establish any kind of independent life. The pressures of conforming to what he expected of me meant life was too false and stressful to be truly enjoyable. He never knew what really went on in my life when he was not around, or how I thought about myself. I could never see myself as a beauty: although the mirror told me my face looked good I was disgusted by the rest of my body which I could only see as fat and awful. My overwhelming desire was to be slim, and thoughts about eating filled my entire life. I didn't know in those days that there were such people as compulsive eaters, but there is no doubt that I was a classic example. A compulsive eater is somebody who is out of control about food, they go on diets and then the control breaks and they stuff themselves with food, feel guilty and depressed about what they have done, and eat more to compensate for that depression. After a while they snap out of it, start dieting again – and so it goes on.

My cycle was the four-day trap, one I now see quite often in my clients at the Maisner Centre. For four days I would starve myself, nibbling just the occasional lettuce, tomato and boiled egg, then I would break down into bingeing, stuffing down anything that I could find to eat until I felt so sick I couldn't move. One of my great weaknesses was condensed milk. It was not possible to get fresh milk in Spain in those days so Evaristo used to bring me catering-sized tins of sticky sweet condensed milk. I can see myself now guzzling down great spoonfuls of the stuff until the huge tin was empty and I felt quite sick. But it was more than a physical sickness I suffered from. I felt disgusted with myself, my whole personality was distorted by my addiction to eating, just as an alcoholic or a drug addict is somebody different once their addiction has them in its grip.

But on the surface nothing of this showed. When Evaristo called round I would make sure I had stopped eating, when we went out to dinner I picked daintily at my food, then when I was at home alone I would stuff myself with any food I could find. He could not really have guessed I had an eating problem, he never saw me do more than toy with my food, and from photographs of myself taken at that time I know I was not overweight. I managed to keep slim in spite of my food bingeing because I was also completely hooked on speed and laxatives. Amphetamines were easy to get hold of and I was soon swallowing doses up to ten times those prescribed. Not only did I have trouble sleeping with all that speed racing around my system, but after a while the pills no longer seemed to be working on suppressing my appetite. I know now that compulsive eating has little to do with physical appetite. It is more to do with physical or emotional needs, or both. Of course a starving person will binge, as will someone suffering from low blood sugar levels, certain food allergies, and other physical disorders. But in many cases the reasons for food addiction lie at an emotional and psychological level.

Like all compulsive eaters I became obsessed about the size of my stomach. I was always convinced it was huge and stuck out in an ugly way, so I used to take vast amounts of laxatives to try to reduce it. Taking large doses of laxatives is one aspect of a condition called bulimia nervosa, the medical name for purging the body, either by taking laxatives, or making yourself sick, or both.

Bulimia becomes a habit. Many girls discover by accident that they feel better after vomiting if they have been bingeing. They begin by telling themselves they will not do it again, or just occasionally, but they soon find they are doing it more and more until in some cases they have to vomit after every meal. I remember being surprised to discover that there was a medical name for what I did, and also that 'normal' people did not do it. With me, eating and purging became linked in my mind quite early on, and like most bulimics I became hooked on the habit, even though it was wrecking my health and ruining my life.

Those who constantly make themselves sick develop a range of other problems. Acid from the vomit rots the teeth, the strain of repeated vomiting causes all sorts of physical discomfort, while laxatives cause haemorrhoids and severe intestinal disorders. The chemical balance of the body is completely destroyed, which has a long-term effect on organs like the liver and kidneys. The stomach actually gets bigger, thus defeating the original purpose of the purging. But even knowing all the grim facts, a bulimic finds it impossible not to think about emptying her stomach as soon as food is put into it. In time it is not just the uncomfortable full feeling after a binge that prompts purging, but even the smallest snack triggers the urge to throw it all back out.

Although the people who met me in those days in Spain must have thought – if they thought about me at all – that I led a rather glamorous life with plenty to please me and little to worry about, in fact, because of the tortured state of my personality during that period, things were very different. Life in the shadow of a personality such as Evaristo was either sky high or down in the depths. The knowledge that he had whole areas of his life where I did not belong, which included his wife and home and his office and business, tore great holes in me. The anticipation of waiting for his call, the agony when he didn't come, the constant tension when he was with me that I might do or say something to upset him so he would walk out and leave me alone again, put me under constant pressure. He was my whole life so I made no other real friends and I rarely went out alone in case I wasn't there when he called. It was a way of life that fitted snugly with my compulsive eating habits, the emotional ups and downs matched by food blow-outs and famines.

One day Evaristo set out on a trip to Germany and simply disappeared. Nobody ever heard from him again. I have no idea what happened to him, whether he died or just turned his back on everything and started a fresh elsewhere. Of course I was devastated. Not only had I lost the man I worshipped but I was left alone with a small child, penniless in a foreign country. It wasn't long before I became seriously ill with hepatitis, and it took me a long time to crawl back to anything like living again.

Once again, with Evaristo I had got myself into a negative relationship – not that it seemed like it at the time, but in those days I did not stop to analyse my behaviour. I was totally unaware of why I did or did not do things, which is probably why so many details of my life have completely vanished from my memory. It is easier to talk about negative relationships than positive ones; negative ones are those that are not really working, there is plenty to grumble and complain about, and they lead to all sorts of anti-social behaviour. My idea of a positive relationship between parents and children is one where the parents give emotional support where it is needed and listen to their children and communicate with them. In so many cases, however, parents put a great load on their children, either by just not caring and communicating enough or by trying to live their own lives through their children and not being able to let go.

One good example of this is Sarah. Both her parents were doctors and it was always their intention for her to follow in the family tradition. But Sarah did not manage to pass the necessary exams for medical school so to try to please her parents she went into nursing instead. The fact that she did not like the work and it just made a misery of her whole life was never communicated to her parents and she continued to live with it until her mid-30s, by which time her eating and drinking problems had reached such a pitch she was forced to stop and take stock of her life. She realised it was time to make far-reaching changes, and that was when she began to study art and found something fulfilling and worthwhile for herself.

For so many people the years just pass by – wasted years in a lot of cases because the negative is easier to sustain than the positive is to create. I am thinking of Ray who drank heavily for years: he lost his driving licence and on the very day he got it back, went out drinking, drove home and got stopped again. He decided it was time to stop drinking at last, but the main problem he came up against was that all his friends were drinkers, or rather that he spent so much time in pubs and bars he did not know anybody who did not drink. His way of getting out of the drink trap was to make a different kind of friendship, so that a glass of alcohol was no longer an integral part of his social life. I can relate to Ray's experience because I found I began mixing with a different and far more interesting crowd of people when I eventually decided to give up drinking. I discovered many of my drinking friendships were not as genuine as I had believed; hard drinkers, like drug addicts or compulsive eaters, are too tied up in their own problems to leave much room for others.

Friendship has to be a two-way thing, but so many are just a one-way street, one person gives and the other takes. These days I am better at recognising when I am getting into a negative sort of relationship; I feel tired and drained if the other person is taking and taking and giving little in return. It was put very well by one of my clients who wrote to me describing her battle to get back to a normal way of life: 'Passive dependent people are so busy seeking to be loved that they have no energy left to love. They are like starving people scrounging wherever they can for food and with no food of their own to give to others.'

If we don't love ourselves, how can we ever expect others to love us for ourselves alone? That is how people become what I call 'people pleasers', they try to buy the love and attention of others because they are unable to believe it is something that can be freely given. They pay out and pay out, sometimes with money to buy gifts, drinks, luxuries, sometimes by laying themselves down as a doormat to be trampled by others, sacrificing their own wants and needs to please someone else. There are plenty of people who are prepared to please others whatever the cost to themselves. I should know – I was one of them for long enough. It is another of those states which are ready and waiting for people with low self-esteem to drop into. But it isn't long before people begin to take advantage of you, and then you start to feel used and your self-esteem drops even lower.

I remember with so much affection Aunt Dolly, who loved me unconditionally. I suppose she was the ultimate 'people pleaser' because she only saw the side of me she wanted to see and never recognised my faults. She was not actually my aunt but a childless lady quite a bit older than me who in a way adopted me when I was living in Spain. We met one day at a bus stop, she was ill and alone and so I helped her home and we became friends. Although she was teetotal herself, she used to come round the bars with me in the evenings after I finished work. She was lonely and prepared to sit and watch me downing the booze night after night for the sake of my company. Yet in spite of that she would solidly declare that she had never seen me drunk; I can only think that because she had never seen me sober she had no way of knowing the difference!

In those days when I was young and irresponsible I never stopped to think about what I was doing or how I felt. Because I took no responsibility for myself, when things went wrong I just blamed other people. That sort of attitude makes any kind of long-term relationship doomed to failure, although immature and irresponsible living can seem exciting and attractive to an outsider at first meeting. It is so easy to blame everyone else for your own failures, which is why any alcoholic, bulimic or drug addict will soon come up with stories of how others have let them down or treated them badly.

When I talk to a client about her eating habits, ask her to talk through her weekly food charts and tell me exactly why she ate that particular cake or spent Friday evening drinking in the pub, too often she will offload responsibility for her actions on to other people. She tells me her mother had baked the cake specially and she did not want to hurt her feelings by not accepting it, that her boyfriend wanted to go to the pub for the evening and insisted she had a drink to keep him company. What is completely lacking in such cases is the self-esteem to stand up and say 'No'. Such people are not taking responsibility for their own lives or communicating their own wants and needs, they are letting others dictate to them.

Yet these people who are always blaming others for their problems are also caught up with a lot of guilt. The two negative states are closely linked, feelings of guilt prevent self-assertion, lack of self-assertion leads to the doormat personality. Most feelings of guilt come from within; from criticising one's own actions it is a short step to taking everything other people say as criticism.

It is only since I have grown confident enough to say what I want and don't want from others that I have come to realise most people appreciate such straightforwardness. It is so much easier to get on with other people, whether on a casual basis or in a close relationship, if you are honest with each other. Then each one knows where they stand and is not being drawn into elaborate guessing games. It still takes me by surprise sometimes to find just how tolerant people are if you state how you feel clearly and honestly.

Only the other day I had a flat full of visitors, working and doing courses with me over the weekend. By Sunday afternoon it was getting on top of me and it showed in the way I was prowling around, picking things up and putting them down and not really paying attention to what anyone was saying. Then someone said, 'Paulette, why don't you sit down and ask yourself what you really want?' So I did, and told them I just wanted a bit of time on my own. They all packed me off for a walk; they were probably glad to be rid of me in my restless mood. I appreciated the break from them, and nobody was the slightest bit offended. At one time I would never have allowed people to think I did not want to be in their company constantly, in case they were hurt. I would have been making an assumption not based on fact, I would have brooded on it inside and become more and more stressed until I went off and had a huge binge, which of course would have been blamed on them. In too many people there is an inability to express any resentment they feel, it is just left to build up and up. In this way relationships become closed and estranged and an effort must be made to open them up before misunderstandings become too deeply entrenched to be swept aside.

Where an unhappy relationship sparks off compulsive behaviour, before long that very behaviour makes future good relationships with others an impossibility. Ron was lonely after his marriage broke up and began drinking heavily, at first because he could find company in pubs and bars, and later because he became hooked on drink. One night he met a girl in a bar. They spent hours drinking together and he soon became convinced that she was the one who was going to make him happy again. But she had a drink problem too, she drank because she found life difficult to cope with. Things were fine when they were out together at the pub or at home sharing a few drinks in bed, but she found it hard to handle things like meeting Ron's parents or waiting at home for him to get back from work. Before long she was drifting on to the next man she met over a casual drink. Ron was so desperate to meet someone to share his life with him that he was blind to her shortcomings, and she so needed someone to give her a sense of security she refused to see his problems.

I see so many clients who are so desperate for love and for something to cling to that they make martyrs of themselves, often without realising they are doing it. They actually deny themselves happiness and a life of their own for the sake of others. They place a terrible burden on the victims of this martyrdom, and sometimes the woman herself is the victim.

When I lived with Joe I suppose I was so desperate for him to love me and see me as perfect that I never went out or had any kind of life of my own. I didn't see myself as a martyr but I suppose that was what I was trying to do, saying, 'Look what I am giving up for you'. But he probably never even noticed. I knew when I met him that he had a drink problem, but I've always had a tendency over the years to tie myself up with alcoholics, so this was nothing new. I thought he would improve if I was there to look after him, but he still disappeared on benders leaving me just sitting alone at home. One year we had been invited to a friend for Christmas, but Joe went out drinking on Christmas Eve and didn't sober up for four days. I just sat at home all over Christmas waiting for him to become coherent enough to notice me. It never occurred to me to leave him to it and go off to my friend's alone. I was too afraid he would blame me, would throw me out, would not love me any more, so I let him behave like that and never spoke a word of criticism.

Women are notorious for believing they will change a man once they are married or in a permanent relationship with him. They turn a blind eye at first to little faults or annoying habits, convinced they will soon manage to eradicate them, but as time goes on these things not only don't go away, they grow and cause friction in the relationship. A client of mine came for help because she said she was so overweight her husband told her he found her repulsive. She took it from him, blamed herself, felt she was ugly and fat and tried to lose weight, but the more desperate she was to diet the more weight she put on because she could not stop bingeing due to her unhappy life. Their relationship was a mess, she just let her husband put her down all the time and she no longer remembered that he had been just as bad years ago when she weighed only nine stone. He suffered from huge inadequacies and took it out on her, but while she was prepared to take all the guilt on herself she had no hope of coming to terms with the real problems in the relationship, which were largely in her husband's personality.

The bottom line is that someone in a bad relationship that is unlikely to improve has two choices, they can either get out or they can alter their attitude so it does not get to them any more. Time and again I have seen what happens when a wife learns self-assertion after years of being the underdog. When she at last believes she is worth a better kind of life the realisation can break the marriage apart, but usually only where that marriage was not worth saving. Where the relationship is basically sound, if both partners develop true self-esteem they have the chance of building something really worthwhile.

Many of the people I come across in the course of my work come from what is known as dysfunctional families; certainly I can put myself in that category. The definition of a dysfunctional family is one where one or both parents have a compulsive problem such as alcoholism, or some other obsession that limits their lifestyle to rigid boundaries and prevents them from showing affection. I believe that a lot of people who suffer from chronic depression also have this kind of background. It may be years of seeing father dead drunk every day, or the fear and guilt instilled in the household of a hellfire preacher that in time take their toll.

Although the theory of dysfunctional families usually proves true, still 90 per cent of my clients start off by saying they come from perfect loving homes; they need to believe it so much that they cannot see their parents as less than perfect. As they get better and more in control of their own lives the scales begin to drop from their eyes and they can see their parents for what they are, human beings with faults and weaknesses just like everyone else. Anyone who is hooked on a relationship, whether it is with parents, children, husband, boyfriend or whoever, cannot see things clearly, they only see what they want to see.

Some fortunate infants from secure, stable homes seem to know instinctively many of the relationship skills which it has taken me years to learn. Because I was never taught as a child to cope with people and to form real relationships it has been a hard struggle.

As my attitude to others has changed and my own self-esteem has improved I am better able to communicate and interact with others, and as I constantly tell my clients this is the only way to achieve real, lasting relationships. There are no short cuts.

AUTOMATIC REACTION

My secretary did not have to ask if something was wrong: as soon as she spotted the watering can in my hand she knew I had a problem, so she tactfully retired to her typewriter while I began the lengthy task of watering my plants. Over the years I have been given or otherwise acquired dozens of indoor plants, they have almost taken over the living room of my flat which doubles as an office. I have got into the habit, every time something annoys or upsets me, or when I feel under stress or have a problem, of pottering off to water my plants. I find the positive action of tending my leafy friends calms my mind and helps me get the situation back under control.

Like most people, I have developed habitual ways of responding to situations, especially stressful ones, but up until recent years those habits were usually bad ones. Over the years it became almost automatic to react to rejection or failure by going on a binge or on the booze. At one period of my life it was my habit to react to the feeling of not being able to cope by downing pills to 'pep me up'.

When I recently began to be more aware of the sort of responses I was making to situations and to think in a more positive way about my life, I asked myself why my habitual responses should always be negative actions. If a habit is something one does almost without realising it, what an opportunity this presents for making changes. By retraining negative habits to positive ones, life will automatically become more fulfilling.

As a child I sucked my thumb and bit my nails. Nothing too terrible about that, lots of children do it. But then when I went to school the things I did got worse: for example, I was always asking to go to the toilet so I could rummage through other children's coat pockets in the cloakroom and steal their sweets. The awful thing about it all was that nobody seemed to care about me enough to notice, much less take this behaviour as a sign of my deep-seated unhappiness. Over and over again as I grew up I was allowed to develop these behaviour patterns, as if I was being encouraged to look for an easy way out all the time rather than face up to the human realities of the person I was growing to become.

Good habits tend to be the sort of thing we never give any thought to; washing your hands after going to the toilet, or brushing your teeth before you go to bed, are automatic actions. Good manners like saying thank you, replying to letters, opening doors, are usually the result of habits acquired during childhood which may once have been a struggle to perform but which in time become second nature. It is bad habits that get all the attention when they annoy or inconvenience other people or make us feel guilty or ashamed. Just think how many smokers light up when they make themselves a cup of coffee, how many children switch on the television as they walk in the door from school. Every now and then these sorts of things are highlighted as bad habits, but because they do not appear to be very harmful and it is an effort to change established patterns, few people make much effort to change.

Then there are the bad habits which are in fact entrenched attitudes of mind, negative thoughts and actions which at worst can completely destroy lives. Take workaholism: so many people slip into the habit of making pressure of work an excuse for not really making any sort of life or relationships for themselves. It can destroy a marriage when one member of the family becomes a stranger in their own home, with the knock-on effect on the rest of the family. Often all there is to show for all that effort is money – and sometimes not even that – but the workaholic gets little pleasure from his wealth as he has lost the habit of knowing how to enjoy himself. He is so deeply caught up in the habit of work, work, work, that the rest of the world hardly seems to exist.

Nowadays, if I'm asked 'When did you last enjoy yourself?' I don't find it hard to come up with an answer. I enjoy my daily swims at the nearby pool, my trips to the theatre or out to dinner with friends.

At the Maisner Centre I find clients have slipped into the habit of automatically bingeing or starving in response to certain situations, so the first thing I ask them to do when they begin a course with me is to fill in daily charts every time they eat something. These charts are a record not only of what they eat but also when, where and what mood they were in at the time. When I next see that person I look through the charts and try to assess what sort of patterns are emerging. Often only when a client sees an habitual pattern written down can they recognise it and become aware of just what they are doing. They can then work out ways of putting problems right.

For example, Julia binges regularly every Saturday fortnight, which is directly connected with the fact that her in-laws, with whom she doesn't get on, come to visit every second Sunday. Over the years it has become a habit for her to get herself worked up over their approaching visit and turn to food to relieve the stress. In a case like this where a binge can be directly associated with some habitual response to a certain situation, the way to get the bingeing under control is to alter the habit. Basically Julia has such negative feelings towards her in-laws and their visits that she has developed the bad habit of dreading their arrival. She realised that she had to work on changing her response to the situation before she would get her Saturday binges under control.

In many situations people say to me that they only eat when they are bored, to which the obvious answer is to do something about the boredom. Flopping out in front of the television or just sitting about doing nothing is fine if you enjoy it and feel better for a relaxing break. But if you do it because you can't think of anything better to do to pass the time, you aren't enjoying the programmes and are feeling bored, it is hardly surprising that thoughts of food begin to creep into your mind and commercial breaks become an excuse to visit the food cupboard. Sitting around doing nothing, being bored and feeling bad about it, can become a habit in itself, but just trying to get rid of a bad habit like that is extremely difficult because of the vacuum it leaves. Which is why most people usually give up trying and soon slip back into their old ways. The trick is to develop good habits to replace the bad ones, in other words, start doing something so that you don't have time left to be bored and dissatisfied. Whatever the bad habit is, it probably takes up quite a chunk of your life, so it will be essential to fill that gap if you decide to chuck the habit out. Which is why I now water my plants, or do a crossword, when I feel stressed instead of bingeing or even sitting around fighting the urge to binge.

Here is another way of training yourself to turn bad habits into good habits which I recommend to many of my clients. On one of those good days when you are feeling on top and motivated to make changes, get ten pieces of paper and write on each something that you like to do such as having a bubble bath, walking the dog, arranging a vase of flowers. Fold up each piece of paper and put them all in a handy pot, then on the down days when you can't face anything and know a binge is looming, take a paper out of the pot and act on what it says.

Just as bad habits are learnt, so good habits can also be acquired if you put your mind to it. But the person who lets their bad habits run away with them could be the type of personality who needs to keep their good habits under control as well. The compulsive person can so easily allow a habit to become an obsession.

I am thinking in particular of a girl I once shared an office with; I always admired the disciplined way she made sure her appearance was immaculate. She did her make up and hair faultlessly before she left home in the morning and made repairs at regular intervals during the day. She was the sort of girl who never had a hair out of place no matter what, and I often envied her willpower and control. Some time later I heard a story about her which showed me her attention to her appearance was nearer an obsession than a good habit. One evening the police telephoned her to say her boyfriend had been involved in an accident and they were afraid he might be dying, could she come to the hospital immediately. Instead of rushing to his bedside, she made excuses to delay because even in that situation she could not step outside the door without re-doing her make-up and changing her clothes.

When it comes to food habits, so many people let their ideas about what they should and should not eat become obsessions rather than sensible guides. Calling in at the chip shop every single day is not really a good habit, especially for someone with health or weight problems. But on the other hand there is nothing wrong with the occasional fish and chip supper if you enjoy it. It is all a matter of striking a balance, of adapting behaviour to what is appropriate for the occasion. Having a drink on a social occasion is appropriate in our society, it is only when alcohol becomes an obsession and drinking begins to take over as a way of life that the real dangers start. If such obsessive habits are used as a way of expressing emotion because the natural channels of expression are blocked, that person has a real problem.

Because I never learnt openness, warmth, and communication from my parents, it never came naturally to me to show openness and warmth to others.

In between the early years 'locked' alone in my bedroom and the present satisfaction with my own company and the welcome visitors who frequently call round for dinner parties or Scrabble evenings, I can look back on so many guilty years of lone bingeing and boozing sessions shut away from the world. Like all compulsive eaters my food orgies were very private affairs, I would manipulate times to be alone so that I could binge and binge in secret. I see so many girls like Sandra who initially binged because her husband went out to play football every Saturday and didn't come home until late. She blamed him for going out and leaving her alone, but in time she began to encourage him to go so that she could be alone to binge. His football gave her an excuse to eat alone. Once compulsive eating gets a hold it changes your whole attitude to life.

It is very easy to find excuses for not dealing with situations: anything from poor health to blaming one's parents for bringing you up wrongly. At one time it became a habit with me to say I had an eating problem because my parents did not love me, and to believe I had a drink problem because nobody had taught me how to handle relationships successfully. Now I can see far more clearly that my problems were largely of my own making, that I allowed myself to use my unhappy childhood as an excuse for dreadful behaviour as an adult. I just slipped into that comfortable way of thinking where everything is someone else's fault and I was just the poor victim. From there it was easy to adapt every misfortune to fit my patterns of thought. It was this way of thinking that I eventually had to get to grips with and change; nothing will ever change the historical facts of my past.

The trouble was that these thought patterns became so familiar, and anything familiar is comfortable for its own sake. The thought itself is painful but the way of thinking is easy. The difficulty is getting out of that comfortable rut, and often it takes an outsider to suggest how this can be done. When I was younger there were not the same opportunities to seek out professional help as there are today. There was nothing like the Maisner Centre to help me recognise and come to terms with my compulsive eating habits, and nobody to point me towards self-assertiveness courses because I doubt if such things even existed. I can sometimes suggest to my clients ways of tackling their problems which they would never have thought of, because I am an outsider seeing their situation as a whole rather than being on the inside trying to peer out.

Helen was such a case, she was a chronic bulimic and as I have already mentioned bulimia is a very habit-forming sort of complaint. Helen had done well on the Maisner course and was very much on the way to overcoming her eating problems, but breaking the bulimia habit was proving difficult, until I suggested a method which worked amazingly well. First of all I told her that she was not to allow herself to vomit during the week, but could do so at 11 am. on Sunday mornings. This took a lot of the pressure off giving it up altogether, a prospect which she found terrifying and secretly believed she would never be able to do. With 'Sundays off' she had something to hold on to during the week. She told herself she would not vomit today, just two more days to go – just one more day – and suddenly she had succeeded in getting through the whole six days. But then I added that she *had* to make herself sick on Sunday mornings. It was an order, but surprisingly she found this very difficult to do. So from trying not to vomit seven days a week she was now trying to do it one day a week – and struggling. The habit had been successfully broken and in the end she was able to put bulimia nervosa behind her.

A rather more subtle kind of emotional habit which I come across time and again not only with my clients at the centre but with people in all walks of life, is that insidious habit of always blaming yourself for everything that goes wrong. I used to do this myself too – it was closely linked with the idea of blaming everyone else for my misfortunes, the two are just opposite sides of the same coin. If I applied for a job and did not get it I would think there was something terribly wrong with me, without considering that 500 other people had also applied for the same job. Whenever the latest man in my life left me I drowned myself in self pity, telling myself I was not worthy of anybody liking me.

I can associate this habit of thinking with the feelings of guilt my parents instilled into me for the way I looked, the way I behaved, the way I stood and walked and sat and generally existed. When my marriage broke up there was heavy disapproval, remarks that there had never been a divorce in the family before, how would they explain it to other people, the worry and shame was putting years on them. I don't remember them ever once asking if I was unhappy, if I needed help and support, if I had been treated badly. On top of the anguish of my own life falling apart around my ears and my automatic reaction of blaming myself for everything that had gone wrong, I was loaded up with the guilt at what the situation was doing second-hand to my family.

Those who play on the emotions of others in this way don't realise the sort of damage they can be doing. Doreen, one of my clients, told me she was having dreams about her mother dying, and on talking it through I discovered that her mother had actually died many years earlier when Doreen was quite young. It had been her mother's habit whenever Doreen was naughty to tell her off and sigh and say Doreen would be the death of her. She probably only used it as a figure of speech, but one day Doreen came home late from playing with a friend, expecting her mother to be angry, but finding the doctor at their house. Her mother had suffered a severe heart attack that afternoon and never recovered. Somewhere in Doreen's mind she made the connection that she had been the death of her mother by being naughty, just as her mother had always promised, and years later she was still unable to rid herself of the burden of guilt.

Rummaging through some old papers recently I came across a letter I wrote to myself as a way of releasing myself from the feelings of guilt which were weighing me down and causing me so many problems. I had been out to a party and met someone who worked as a therapist with drug addicts. During the conversation he talked about this method of forgiving yourself for things you feel guilty about, and as it coincided with the time when I was beginning to find ways of sorting myself out I decided to go home and give it a try.

Here is the letter I wrote. As I re-read it it still holds a deep significance for me, and I can picture myself at three in the morning pacing up and down the kitchen, pen in hand, scribbling, jotting and screwing up page after page until I had something I felt was near enough to how I was feeling.

Dear Paulette,
I am sorry I have spent so many years
ignoring your real needs and wants; no wonder
you have become so resentful.
I am sorry I spent so many years running
away from the real Paulette, trying to hide
behind other people or getting lost in food,
and drink and pills. I will try to put you
first from now on and understand what you really
want from life.
I am sorry I blamed you for being a lazy
slob, when really you were just tired out and
depressed. I am sorry I believed you were
aggressive and unpleasant, when really you
were just too shy to make proper friends.
I am sorry I was angry at all the
mistakes you made, when more often than not
you were the victim of your childhood.
I am sorry, I hated you so much for
sometimes being cruel to your son when you
did not have the resources or the knowledge

to be a mature parent.
From today onwards I will give you the
love you deserve, which I have continually
denied you in the past.
Your loving friend,

Paulette

Of course I didn't change overnight or throw off a lifetime's guilt in a few paragraphs, but the act of writing down how I felt about myself, and forgiving myself, was a significant step forward on my road to recovery.

Now during my sleepless nights I remind myself that the small hours are when I get my best ideas. In other words I have taught myself the new habit of finding a positive side to a negative thought. Recently I had a telephone call out of the blue from a top psychiatrist who asked if I would be prepared to give a talk about compulsive eating to a group of 150 medical people. My first reaction was, 'No, I can't do it', but before I had a chance to say this I told myself that if I was not up to doing it this important man would not have gone to the trouble of asking me. So I started to turn over plans in my mind to draw up comprehensive lecture notes and brush up on my public speaking techniques. By the time I had stopped shaking with anxiety over the invitation I was quivering with anticipation at the excitement of the challenge. I have taught myself that when a difficult challenge comes along I must remind myself that it is only my way of thinking that is holding me back from doing anything in the world that I want to do.

MAKING CHANGES

One hot Spanish evening I finished work, went home to change and then met up with Aunt Dolly for one of our usual evenings around the local bars. Things were much as usual, she had her cup of tea and I ordered a large vodka, and we sat at a table in the corner where a gentle finger of evening breeze took the edge off the sultry heat. I don't remember what we were talking about, whether it was of any particular significance, but halfway through that drink I suddenly pushed it away and announced that I was not going to drink any more. I didn't touch alcohol again for a year.

Anyone who has tried and tried to give up drinking and always failed will say how lucky I was to be able to give up just like that. In a way I suppose I was, I had few withdrawal symptoms and felt a lot better, but I know that stories of instant conversions such as that are very few and far between. I can now recognise that I was not cured of my alcohol addiction, just rigidly controlling it by sheer force. Years later when I really got to grips with curing myself of my drinking problem altogether it was much, much more difficult.

I had recognised that I was totally controlled by my drinking by then, it dictated how I led my life and how I filled my days, or rather my evenings and nights, and I felt I wanted to be back in control of my own life. But to maintain that control I had to restrict my whole life, so I did not go anywhere or do anything. I could not go out socially because everyone else would be drinking, so I became lonely and isolated and the quality of my life was not improved. In fact, inside I felt far worse than in the days when I could drown all my problems and miseries and forget them for a while. It was all rather negative and so it was inevitable that in time I would start drinking again. When I began to crave some sort of social life I started going to discos, and then I would feel the need for a drink overwhelming me because my brain told me that I was too fat to be a disco queen. I would not dance unless I had a few drinks inside me to give me Dutch courage. The occasional drink became regular tipples, and so it crept up and up until I was back to the point where every time I went out anywhere I needed a drink. Once again it was controlling my life, I needed a drink to cope with stress, I needed a drink to cope with boredom. It was not just an emotional prop, I was only physically capable of doing things after a few drinks; it seemed to give me the energy boost to get through the day.

Since then I have come across a lot of 'dry alcoholics': people like Annie, who did not touch a drop for months but who, all the time she was off it, lived with a raging conflict inside her head. She was not cured of her alcoholism, the battle was still going on. Annie had not cured the problems at the root of her need for alcohol. Her self-esteem was so low she felt compelled to be always doing things for other people and never to do anything for herself, but in constantly running round after others she wore herself out and got so tired she found life difficult to cope with. Then a small spark, such as a row at home, would tip her over the edge and she would be off on a bender, straight back to the bottle. She had not learnt to cope with life, nor with the necessity of learning to like herself rather than constantly wearing herself out doing things to try to make other people like her.

It is just the same with compulsive eaters: if they are fighting a battle against eating every moment of the day they have a problem even if they are not actually consuming hundreds of calories. My definition of compulsive eating is not so much to do with the amounts that are eaten but with the *reasons* for eating; if food and eating is an obsession the person has a problem. This theory is borne out by the fact that so many compulsive eaters are not overweight, some are even underweight. They think they look fat and they feel fat, so inside they are fighting a permanent battle against the desire to eat so they can become thinner. That conflict takes over their life and nothing else really matters. Life becomes hell, relationships are shattered, ambition, love, joy and all the good things of life no longer matter, all that matters is food, and eating or not eating.

The compulsive eater's overwhelming desire in life is to be slim, but usually they do not even recognise they have achieved it when they do get to the weight they longed to be. All the other problems are still there so they just redraw the boundaries and carry on trying to get even slimmer in the mistaken belief that then, as if by magic, the quality of their life will improve. I have seen pictures of myself when I was at the height of my obsession during my years in Spain and I did actually have a small waist and slender hips but I know I still thought of myself as fat and hated myself for the way I looked.

Nowadays I have settled down into a weight at which my body seems comfortable, I enjoy buying nice clothes in a size that fits the way I am and I accept that this is more or less the shape and size I am likely to stay for the foreseeable future. No, I am not slender, but I am not huge and obese either, I'm just about right for my age and height. I realise now that the price of an artificially low body weight is more than I am prepared to pay. It cost me dear for many years and at last I am able to say enough is enough.

When I became totally hooked on slimming tablets I was spending every last penny I had on the things, not to mention the hours and hours spent doing the rounds of chemist shops to buy them in sufficient quantities to appease my craving. Although amphetamines are not legally on sale today, it was quite easy in those days to buy speed over the counter, as they were available in Spain without prescription. What long stories I would spin in each shop I visited – how I had lost the last ones I bought, how I was buying them for a friend or a relative. Whether I was believed or not I don't know, and I didn't care, so long as I could walk out with my precious pills. The dubious reward for the huge amount of time and effort spent touring around was that I got to be swallowing a bottle of speed a day when the recommended dose was three tablets.

I became progressively more paranoid, totally sleepless, and it grew more and more difficult to get to work each day. I would fall out of bed, reaching for a handful of pills to wake me up, and struggle out of the house. If I hadn't remembered to wash the night before I would have a quick splash in the ladies room when I got to the office. I was working as a translator, which was a well paid job and high standards were expected, so the only way I managed to struggle through the work was by slipping vodka into my cup every time I visited the Coke machine. Somehow I kept going, in between the alcoholic top-ups and the frequent trips to the toilet, as I was also hooked on large amounts of laxatives which I thought would keep me from getting fat.

I was always getting into fights and arguments. In the evening I would go out drinking and more often than not I would get to a point where something blew my mind and I would lash out. Not surprisingly I was becoming more and more depressed and more and more tired. I had to keep going, keep working and earning, because after Evaristo disappeared and I was alone I was determined to carry on supporting Peter. I worked long hours to pay the fees of a boarding school in Spain called La Salle, one of the most famous schools in the world. In the holidays I paid someone to come from England to teach him English. I felt guilty about sending him away to school but had no choice; he could not live at home while I was out working such long hours. There was little else worth living for except my little boy – but I was thin: for the first time in my life I had the sort of figure I had always dreamed of, and the bitter irony of it was that I didn't even realise what I had achieved.

This is the case with so many of the women I see through the Maisner Centre. Time and again I try to talk to them about sorting out their problems and improving the quality of their life, but I meet the same old brick walls: 'I will think about that when I am slim' or 'I can only think about eating, I can't think about anything else'. I know that if they do lose weight and achieve the thing they are so obsessed about they will still be unhappy and lost because they have not tapped the root of the problem. The continual striving after slimness is escapism: when the mind is full of thoughts of eating there is no room for anything else.

That is how I was, I never stopped to analyse what I was or where I was going, I drifted on from day to day totally in the grip of my drinking, my bingeing, my speed and laxatives, leaving no corner of my mind free for awareness. During my amphetamine years I only felt motivated to take an interest in my appearance if there was a man around to notice me. When I was working in an office of 5,000 men and two women there was some reason to put on make-up and iron my clothes; when I was alone at home I lived like a slob.

Sooner or later the crisis had to come. Nobody can go careering downhill at such a pace for ever without crashing into reality sooner or later. And that is exactly what I did. It had got to the stage where my eyes had trouble focusing, and I was on my way home one night when I ran my car into a lamppost. An ambulance raced me off to hospital, but although I was badly shaken up and rather battered I was not badly hurt. Perhaps the smash had knocked an inkling of sense into me because I asked the friendly hospital doctor to help me get off the amphetamine habit. He took me seriously and locked me in a room for five days of cold turkey. I can't write about that time because it is completely wiped from my memory. It must have been pretty bad but it worked, because it broke my addiction and forced the idea into my brain that slimming pills were not the way to carry on. From that day I started to put on weight again.

There are still a lot of people around caught in the slimming pill trap, even though amphetamines are not freely available any more. I was only 12 when my Harley Street doctor introduced me to them, an age when most people accept without question what those who are supposed to be their elders and betters hand out to them. But at any age it is only too easy to get hooked and not be able to find the way out.

Arabella was one of my numerous clients who had the slimming pill problem. Because the natural sensations of hunger are artificially suppressed the whole system is disorientated, and Arabella had no way of knowing what her body was needing and asking for. She frequently went four days without eating, but her body was starving and at the end of it she went on a huge binge and got very depressed because she was so out of control of her eating.

Learning to eat sensibly is the only way to keep the body functioning efficiently, there are no short cuts. Arabella was so reluctant to give up the pills because she felt they gave her the extra energy she needed for her work and social life; giving up meant going through the hell of feeling totally exhausted. To begin with she could only see the misery of 'coming off'; it was only at a later stage that she was able to realise the rewards of life without speed.

It can take a long time for that message to sink in. Only after trying all the possible escape avenues and coming up against a dead end time and again, does the idea begin to have any real meaning. As long as there appears an easy way of doing things there is little motivation to try the more difficult routes. For so many years I was able to drift along without taking any real responsibility for my life or my body. I could get by and survive even if I was not happy or fulfilled, and I was not prepared to look closely enough at myself to be aware of exactly what I was doing.

It was only when I hit rock bottom in that Spanish hospital ward that I was prepared to ask for help. Up until then I thought I needed my amphetamines and I could not imagine life without them. I looked on them as my friends who helped me through the day so I had absolutely no reason to boot them out of my life. It took a sharp shock such as a car crash to show me that they were not helping me or doing me good. In the same way as it was only after I stopped drinking heavily that I could recognise that my former drinking companions were not really my friends, so it was only after I got off the speed that I could realise how it had been an enemy to my health and sanity. When you are deeply enmeshed in these habits there seems to be no other way of living and therefore there is no motivation to change.

The theory has since been explained to me that three things are needed before a person takes the step of making a change:

● Firstly there must be the right attitude, which of course means realising there is a problem and taking the positive step of wanting to make a change for the better.

● Secondly there has to be knowledge, the practical things like knowing where to get help and learning exactly what changes are possible.

● Finally there is the most difficult step of putting it into practice, and this is where so many good intentions fail unless there is sufficient motivation.

When people do actually make radical changes in their lifestyle it is usually because things have got so bad it is impossible to go on in the old ways, and this provides that shove out of the rut. I didn't care about myself when I was pumping my body full of speed and laxatives and alcohol; only when I was forced to realise my brain was going did I find a reason to pull back. Perhaps I am an exception in that once off the speed I never had a desire to go back on it, but that might have been because I substituted extra booze for the pills and I didn't really get to grips with changing my attitude to life and my lifestyle. Even when I first gave up drinking I did not really alter my basic way of thinking about myself and my life, I just forced myself to survive.

Like most of my clients, I am an all-or-nothing person, so I throw myself totally into my work or whatever else I am involved in. Work has never been too much of a problem to me, I have had any number of good jobs and held on to them, it has always been my personal life that has let me down. The difference between myself today and myself in the past is that now I have a self-esteem which does not let me down, I am in control of my life, not in the grip of food, alcohol or pills. I have learnt when I have a problem to think it through logically instead of running away to hide. I ask myself what is the worst that could happen, and make plans accordingly. Anyone can have bad patches, slip back a bit at times in their journey up from the basement, but once you really decide to climb back things are never quite so bad again. Also, once you have been down and climbed up, the next time you have to make a portion of that journey you know the way. It doesn't make the climb any less difficult but it is never so hard when you are on familiar territory.

When you are on the way up and are sufficiently far to look back on some of your old habits you see them in a different perspective and are unlikely to get so hooked up in them again. For example when I first met Juliana she could not see any way in which she could exist without her habitual eight packs of mints a day. Now she doesn't even think about mints, they are no longer a part of her life. As she overcame her eating problems and her life moved forward step by step, mints became less important. But if she had decided on our first meeting that she would never eat another mint in her life she would have put herself through all kinds of hell. By taking one small step at a time she eventually reached that goal which had once seemed impossibly far-off. It is important to achieve a clear-cut idea of where you are heading. Stop thinking in generalities like 'I'm going to stop bingeing', and start to think about specifics that you can get a real grip on, like 'I am going to an evening class once a week instead of sitting in front of the television eating chocolate.'

You have to know where you are heading and have a reasonable plan of action before you can successfully make changes. There is no benefit in just stopping one thing to replace it with another, like me coming off speed and drinking more to compensate. Nor is there usually any advantage in continually making changes just for the sake of change. A new job, moving house, a change of hairstyle, losing another stone, are not positive steps unless they are the expression of changes that are being made within. If you don't like yourself with brown hair you will soon feel equally dissatisfied if you become a redhead; if you have an unhappy life in one house you won't improve things by packing all your problems with your luggage and moving on. Only if you grow to like yourself more, and have more respect for yourself as a person, will you really make a change for the better.

I see how I drifted along for all those years, from one job to another, one country to another, one bar, one man, one problem to another, always in search of something better and never realising the germ of what I wanted was inside me all the time. At any moment in our lives we can find ourselves standing on a bridge. We cannot stay on that bridge for ever, we have to either move on or go backwards. I have stepped on and off that bridge for years, forever running back to the protection of my obsessive habits and never, until comparatively recently, actually crossing over and discovering a completely new way of life on the other side. When I meet people at drug centres or assess my own clients, I can recognise those who have moved forward and those who have stepped backwards from their own personal bridge.

Jacqueline has been trying to stand still in her relationship with Fred for years. She has a big house and a huge weight problem, Fred is an alcoholic. He drained her of money and emotion but she could not break away from him because every time she tried she was pulled back by the overwhelming fear of loneliness. She came to me because she had convinced herself that if she lost weight she would be able to handle Fred and his problems. In time she realised that he would still be an alcoholic even if she lost ten stone, he would just carry on dragging her down as long as she let him, no matter what size she was. Finally she made the step forward of confronting Fred and telling him unless he made a real effort to control his drinking she would not give him any more money. The change she made was believing in herself more, finding the self-esteem to believe she was worth more than the lifestyle Fred and his drinking was imposing on her.

You don't make changes until you say to yourself – and believe it – 'I am worth more than this and I deserve better'. For too many years I was prepared to settle for second best; now I have established a viable business of my own and achieved something worthwhile. I am really in the driving seat, not continually on a knife edge in case my personal life runs out of control and wrecks my business career. That is what happened when I had a second-hand furniture shop in Spain. The business was successful and I had some wealthy and famous clients, like the famous American writer Chester Himes. He came in one day to buy a reproduction desk from me for a villa he was having built in Spain. The villa was a disaster and he got involved in lengthy court cases over it, so he moved me into his home to translate all the correspondence and documents. He was a successful man in many fields, a great friend of Martin Luther King, and he would have been an influential ally for me, but we fell out because I was always getting drunk. With all the money I was earning from the furniture shop going on food, alcohol and amphetamines, I was never in a position to expand and move forward. My partner was as bad as me in her way; she used to embarrass me by getting drunk and falling about in bars, yet despite our high-flying social life we always managed to turn up for work on time each day.

We were able to keep things looking acceptable on the outside – I am sure our customers never realised what we got up to outside working hours. But that is almost the hallmark of the compulsive person, they become experts at deception and hiding the truth, sometimes even from themselves. I have met quite a few bulimics who were only driven to try and make changes when they began to suffer from things that others might notice, like their hair falling out or their teeth rotting. They had gone on for years wrecking their insides but carried on and on vomiting as long as it could be kept secret.

It took me 40 years to reach the point when I was really ready to make changes, and even then it was a slow and painful process. For years and years I had just gone round and round in circles making the same mistakes time and again. Things went rapidly downhill until the car crash that led to my getting off speed, but I was drinking heavily and not in control of my life; I needed someone to cling on to.

Hutch was an Englishman. He had designed the prototype of a beach buggy and come over to Spain to develop it. Because of my language skills he got me to do a lot of translating for him to help with his work, and we started living together. They were hard times for us both, but happy and good times because we shared them. Soon after we met there was a postal strike in Britain and Hutch was not receiving any money from the people sponsoring his work. I was also out of work so we could spend long hours together, although we hardly shared a penny between us, work on Hutch's car more or less came to a halt. A favourite way of passing the day was to put our heads together over word games and crossword puzzles in newspapers pinched from hotels after the guests had finished reading them. We had time to spend with Peter, who adored Hutch and told me he wanted him to be his father. I think that was a happy time for

Peter as well; although he had few toys he could amuse himself building castles out of sand and stones or throwing a ball about on the beach with Hutch and me.

I was very much in love. I saw Hutch as the man who was going to rescue me at last from myself, someone with so much self confidence he had plenty to spare to compensate for my own severe lack of self-esteem. While we were poor we were happy, because it drew us closer together and I had Hutch totally for myself. But then our finances improved and the cracks in our relationship began to show, the arguments started, and in the end Hutch walked out. He never told me exactly why he was leaving, or if he did it did not sink in. I suppose it was my drinking that drove him away; I know we used to have arguments about it, he would say I drank too much and I would deny it, mainly because I had been so drunk the night before I didn't remember what I had said or done. Although I did know I was consuming a lot of drink it just did not occur to me that I had a drink problem. Nowadays I know this is a very common state of mind in people with compulsive disorders. The other day I was at the drug and alcohol abuse centre and a middle-aged man was vehemently denying he was an alcoholic. 'I haven't got a drink problem, 'he repeated over and over again, 'I have cut my drinking down to five or six pints a night, I don't need to be here.'

'Why do you come then?' someone asked, and bit by bit the story came out. His probation officer sent him along to the group because he was continually in trouble for getting into fights when he was drunk. His doctor also insisted he came since a recent spell in hospital when he had been admitted suffering from the DTs.

'But I haven't got a drink problem,' he insisted. Out of the same mould came a new client who telephoned me to start doing a course with the Maisner Centre. 'Are you a compulsive eater or are you bulimic?' I asked. 'I am a compulsive eater, I only make myself sick occasionally,' she said.

'But you do make yourself sick. That is bulimia,' I said.

'I am not bulimic,' she insisted. 'I only make myself sick to stop myself from putting on weight.'

That was the very attitude I used to have. It could have been me saying I don't have a drink problem, I just like a few drinks. It never registered with me how my constant drinking was disrupting my whole life, how my days revolved around drinking and its after-effects.

I would beg Hutch to take me out in the evenings, promising wildly that if he did I would not drink. Then when we got where we were going I would have 'just one', and then another and another until I had slipped back into my cosy fog where all the sharp corners of reality were softened. Next morning the arguments would begin again. Being in love made no difference to my drinking, any more than it prevented my food binges. I used these props not just to fill in empty gaps in my emotional life but to patch over the vast areas of my personality that totally lacked inner resources to handle life with confidence. It was easier to live a life with nothing to lose, because when I had something worth keeping the sheer terror of possibly losing it made life a nightmare of insecurity. I was so afraid of losing Hutch I actually created the very situation which eventually drove him away. I still had not learnt how to handle a relationship in a mature adult way.

My mind went spinning down the same old track, that if I was slim he would love me more, so I was forever starting to diet to achieve that ideal figure, starving myself until my body demanded food, then I binged, cramming myself with food until I was filled with food and guilt and self disgust, forever racing around the old treadmill in search of that magical slimness that I believed would solve all my problems. When we were really hard up I was not able to drink heavily, we just could not afford it, but I still managed to binge, stuffing myself with fried egg sandwiches in secret, or getting up in the dead of night when Hutch was sleeping to cook flour and water pancakes which I gobbled down greedily.

The stress of being in love was more than I could handle, but when Hutch eventually walked out on me I was completely devastated. In my misery I wanted to blot out reality still further and turned to food and sleeping pills to try and survive the long lonely nights.

One day on my way home from work I called in at the shop where I stocked up on my nightly supply of food goodies ready to binge my way through another 12 hours. I picked up a new glossy novel called Valley of the Dolls – I thought it would be something light to help me pass the sleepless hours before I was next due to appear at my office desk. Someone had mentioned the book to me, saying it was supposed to be based on the life of Judy Garland, a figure to whom I had always felt drawn. Valley of the Dolls is a sordid story of girls whose lives and careers are wrecked by drink and drugs, and I was totally absorbed by the book. It could have been me Jacqueline Susann was writing about. As the night wore on I slumped into such a deep state of depression I could hardly tell where real life ended and fiction began, so I helped myself to a huge overdose from my bottles of 'dolls'.

Some instinct of self-preservation made me pick up the telephone and call my doctor just as I was passing out, and he arrived, closely followed by the Spanish police. By that time I was in a wild state of panic and delirium induced by the drugs, washed down with booze on top of an unstable emotional state. In the confusion I lunged towards a police officer and he went flying headfirst down the stairs. I was promptly arrested.

A turbulent night in the cells was not the end of that particular nightmare; next day I was packed off to a Spanish mental hospital, where among other things they accused me of being on hard drugs and kept me locked away while I underwent treatment. I am still haunted by memories of the electric shock treatment that was routine for many of their patients. It was administered without any kind of sedation or anaesthetic, and patients had to queue up for their turn, watching those in front of them suffering convulsions as the current shot through them. I know these days when this treatment is administered it is done much more humanely, but the horror of what I went through will always be with me.

By the time I had convinced the doctors I was fit to be let out on my own again I was badly shaken up and any shreds of self-esteem I had been clinging on to were completely shot away. Yet even that horrific experience did not kick me out of the pit of a life I was living. I just did not realise what I was doing to myself. It was years before I could look back and see what a mess I had really got myself tangled up in.

But that is the way these things creep up on you. You don't wake up one morning a total wreck, or discover one day that you are miraculously cured of every blemish. The trip to hell and back is long and slow and very painful, and usually it is only when you are well on the homeward journey that you realise just where you have been. The root of my philosophy of life these days is that we all have a choice. We can choose how we live our lives, even how much we choose to be influenced by events and people. The final shaping of our destiny lies in our own hands and each individual is ultimately responsible for himself.

If my Spanish doctor were alive today and reading these words, he would recognise them, because they come from him. 'You can die and leave your son an orphan, or rot in misery for the next 20 years,' he said. 'Or you can choose to start fighting back.' Although a part of me heard what he said and realised that it made sense, at the time I just brushed it all aside. It was as if it all applied to someone else; his advice was valid, but not for me – for some other person. I didn't really listen, but I must have heard, it must have sunk into my mind, because 20 years later the moment arrived when it all came back to me as clear, good sense ... in other words, the penny dropped. I recognise that nearly every idea and concept that I believe in today originated in the talks my doctor and I had together more than 20 years ago.

My doctor was giving me the chance then to choose the difficult task of getting myself together, struggling back to good health and improving the quality of the rest of my life. But I was not ready to hear. I chose to carry on lying there in my easy bed of escapism rather than face up to the daunting task of choosing to do things differently.

I can look back over that whole period and begin to see how it all went so wrong. I just could not handle a full-blown give and take relationship, I was too tangled up in my obsessions with eating and drinking. I tripped over them time and again and fell flat on my face, instead of stepping out confidently and being able to believe in myself. I was like a client of mine who longed to become pregnant, saying the only thing she wanted in life was a baby, and yet she was so caught up in her bulimia she could not stop vomiting even though it was preventing her body from conceiving. In the same way the only thing I wanted in life was Hutch, but I could not shake free of my obsessional behaviour which was presenting us from building a lasting relationship. I could not stop bingeing when I found a man I loved because I had not got to grips with all the things that were so wrong inside myself and were the root causes of my bingeing. Loving someone else was not enough; it was only years later when I learnt to love myself that I finally discovered I could get my eating under control and handle my drinking.

When I was released from the psychiatric hospital I was on my own again. My drinking had got so bad that my doctor thought it would be better for Peter to go back to live with my father in England for a while. I went back to work, and held down various jobs over the following years.

My final job in Spain was working for a wealthy Spanish aristocrat. She had long lived in the shadow of potential kidnappers, and she became the target for bomb attacks by the Basque terrorists. One bomb blew me off my feet when it was thrown into the garden, another went off in the street and I can still feel echoes of the dreadful pain in my ears from the noise of the blast. I decided I had had enough, and as Peter was now grown up and had returned again to England I realised I was lonely in Spain and decided to pack up and return home as well.

MOTIVATION IS DOING SOMETHING

Something amazing and wonderful had happened in Patricia's life, she telephoned me as soon as she got home from work to tell me the momentous news. 'I know you will understand,' she blurted out, breathless with excitement, 'You'll never guess what happened today, I took my jacket off!'

I paused a moment waiting for more, and then my brain clicked over and I remembered the day Patricia came for a consultation with me. She had suffered from eating problems most of her life and for years this had been particularly focused on her arms. She was convinced that fat arms were the cause of all her problems, that was why people did not seem to like her, why she had been passed over for promotion at work, and a dozen other things. For ten years she had always kept her arms covered in public, it had become something of an obsession with her.

Now for two weeks Patricia had been following the Maisner course, filling in charts, following the eating plan and working seriously at getting her eating under control. And here was a real sign that she was moving in the right direction and developing a more realistic view of herself and her life. To anyone who has not suffered in the grip of a compulsive problem it might seem utterly ludicrous to get so excited about a little thing like taking her jacket off. But I knew how much this meant to Patricia and I recognised that she had made one of those small but significant changes which could well mean she had opened the elevator doors and was looking at the climb back up to a happier life.

I am more encouraged when I hear a story like Patricia's than when I get calls from people who announce plans to radically change their whole way of life overnight. Suzanne decided she was enrolling for six aerobics classes a week, Sophia vowed she would never never binge again in her life. I sighed as I listened to these two, then I tried to reason with them and point out that they were trying to do too much too soon, but my arguments fell on deaf ears. Sure enough, after the first two weeks Suzanne felt tired and skipped a class, then believing she had failed totally at aerobics she gave up going to all the other classes. Sophia had a big row with her boyfriend the very next day, ate a packet of biscuits and felt so depressed she followed it up with a full-scale binge. Neither had made any real progress in the long run. Getting better means making changes, but changes have to be gradual, a step at a time, and within the individual's capacity. Suzanne might have stuck to one or even two classes a week and felt good about herself because she was exercising regularly. Sophia, like so many people I see, had to accept that after years of bingeing the chances of it never happening again were pretty remote, especially when faced with a stressful situation. You shouldn't be too hard on yourself, you need to allow yourself the occasional lapse, because it is the ability to learn from those experiences, to pick yourself up and start again, which is really important.

I was well and truly back on the booze again by the time I came back to England. I soon got myself a job and the familiar pattern was re-established, struggling through a day's work and out on benders every night, usually in the company of the other occupants of the house in bed-sitter land where I was based. I did begin to worry when I realised I could not remember events of the previous evening when I surfaced to drag myself to the office each morning, but I kept churning on through the same old familiar rut.

Before long another man came along. It was Joe, the person who was to be the instrument of change in my life, although I did not realise it at the time. Although Joe was an alcoholic he did not drink most of the time, so I didn't drink either. That might sound like a step in the right direction, but in fact I just used to binge even more to compensate. I substituted food binges for booze benders and although things may have looked a bit different on the surface, underneath I still had the same old habits and attitudes.

I did realise things were wrong at this stage so I took the step of going to see a psychiatrist, and he supplied a strong injection of motivation to get better. Before anyone gets the idea that the psychiatrist put me on the right road through his treatment, I must explain that if anything the reverse was the case. After I had mumbled and rambled my way through an explanation of my problems he told me rather pompously that as I had always been fat I should just learn to live with it. Then he gave me a prescription for enough tranquillizers to kill ten people.

'Sod you, you little bastard,' I said to myself as I walked out of his plush consulting rooms. 'I am going to get over my eating problems, just you see if I don't!'

I was angry because he had not understood me, there had been no communication between us, he had not really listened or tuned in to my individual needs. That anger proved a motivation.

The first thing I did in my new self-help programme was to begin keeping records and charts of my eating habits to find out when and why I tended to binge. I had also read up quite a bit about low blood sugar levels and the effect this has on moods and appetite cravings, so I put myself on a special diet suited to victims of low blood sugar levels. From my charts I began to notice that my biggest problem was boredom: when I had nothing to do and little to occupy my mind I would start thinking about eating and before long the urge to binge would overwhelm me.

Then just as I was taking my first steps forward, Joe's business took a step back, which necessitated us spending Monday to Friday each week in London, going back home to Brighton at weekends. I was still bored, and many of my best resolutions slipped out of sight as my mind spun into the familiar old idea that I would get slim first and then I would sort out my other problems. I was very interested in the theory of low blood sugar levels contributing to bingeing and I had it fixed in my mind that I should eat small but frequent protein meals. I found out that the proteins with the lowest calorie levels were egg white and gelatine, so I used to mix up huge amounts of gelatine and orange juice and whip in beaten egg white. I made up this concoction in a large red washing up bowl, throwing away dozens of egg yolks as I only wanted the whites. Through practically living on great spoonfuls of this mixture, well sweetened with Candarel to make it palatable, I actually got down to my goal weight of 7 stone 12 – and I looked dreadful.

People kept saying how ill I looked, my bones stuck out and I had bags under my eyes, but to my ears that was praise indeed, it meant they had noticed I was thin. I didn't realise then that egg white and gelatine are incomplete proteins so I still was not getting proper nutrition.

In this search for slimness I was visiting the gym every day, doing awful exercises on benches, touching my toes and generally suffering agonies. It was all total insanity and I still wasn't getting to grips with my real personal problems, as the drama of the wardrobe illustrated. That was triggered off because as I lost weight I bought myself new clothes in London, but when we came down to Brigton at weekends I had no wardrobe there to hang them in. I never actually said to Joe 'I need a wardrobe, please buy me one'. Instead I was forever ranting and screaming at him, and the lack of wardrobe was behind all our arguments. In my mind I kept on turning over the idea that if he really loved me he would know I needed a wardrobe without my having to ask, therefore he could not possibly love me.

About that time I saw an advertisment in a magazine for a franchise to market a certain slimming method and Joe agreed to buy it for me. We thought it was a double appropriate thing for me to do: it would help me get my eating under control, still the overpowering life's ambition at that time, and also alleviate the boredom of my daily life by giving me a business interest. Although the franchise itself did not come to much it gave me a taste for putting my ideas about eating problems into practical action, which was the first platform on which I later set up the Maisner Centre.

It may have been coincidence that around the same time I saw another advertisement, this time for a course of weekly workshops in personal communication. As I say, it could have been sheer chance, but it might have been that I was beginning to become aware of possibilities for self-improvement and was ready to see the advertisement when it appeared. No doubt dozens of such events had been advertised in newspapers and magazines I had read over the years, but until that period of my life I had never noticed them, much less felt motivated to find out more.

That first workshop was a nightmare for me, I very nearly did not go and finally only made it with the help of a bottle of vodka to numb my terror. I was held back not only by my own shyness, but also by Joe's tacit disapproval. I felt he did not want me to go out and be independent of him. It was a classic situation, one I come across time and again with my clients. I so desperately wanted Joe to love me and look after me I was afraid to assert myself, even to go out and leave him alone, because it might appear I was not lovable enough to deserve what I wanted him to give me. If I acted in an unworthy manner, how could I expect him to carry on loving me? I was sure he would abandon me, leave me alone with my fears and weaknesses again, and so I was obsessed with never doing the slightest thing to upset him. I can see so clearly now what a negative relationship that was, but at the time I was so totally caught up with my own insecurity I was blind to any wider issues.

But some kind of common sense did get the better of me and I started attending those workshops. What an eye-opener it was for me; long before the end of the course I no longer needed the vodka to get me to weekly classes. I was stimulated by the knowledge and insight that was being opened up to me. In one exercise we each had to talk about ourselves for 3 minutes, and I reluctantly admitted I had an eating problem. Instead of receiving sneers and put-downs from the rest of the group, I was astounded to find that in the wake of my confession several others were prepared to admit to the same problem.

From then on I felt compelled to find out just how many other people there were around with my sort of problem. I began to form a self-help group for people with eating problems, because I could see that here was a vast grey area of life that was being totally misunderstood. Here were people who were slim and smart and working at good jobs, who admitted to having real problems with eating – they were the compulsive eaters, something a world apart from those who just eat too much.

Once the bug to join courses began to bite I was eager for more, and the next one I joined was on self-assertiveness. I had never even heard of the subject before, much less attempted to apply it to myself, but if I can pinpoint one particular thing that changed my life I think it must be the discovery of self-assertiveness. My life to date had been a succession of driftings, mainly at the will of others, through a desire to please and placate those I thought would give me love or attention in return. The idea of standing up for myself and saying what I wanted and needed out of life had never really occurred to me. One thing that really stands out about that course is that I realised for the first time how people who, on the surface look quite normal, can have no end of problems. There was a tax inspector there who suffered terrible traumas with his in-laws, but in my ignorance up until then I had never realised tax inspectors could have personal problems, they always seem so confident and in control behind their shiny wooden desks.

From then on I began to look beyond myself and discover what was out there in the world. Things began to fall into place one piece at a time. I was no longer bored because I discovered I could find hobbies and friends to fill my life, and as I began to come out of the shadows I learnt to value myself more and recognise how my own low self-esteem had pinned me down. With these discoveries, which for the first time in my life radically altered my patterns of thinking and my attitude to myself, I also found I no longer needed to drink heavily and I could begin to control the cravings for food which I had been using to fill the empty spaces in my life. The whole process grew like a snowball rolling through crisp, powdery snow. The larger my interest in the outside world became the more I gathered people, work, hobbies and ambitions around me. After the initial push the process gathered its own momentum and each new stage motivated me to move onwards and upwards.

The more I learnt and discovered about myself and other people with eating problems, the more I felt driven to work in this field and create some way of giving constructive help to those with similar problems. At last I had found a positive and worthwhile reason for doing something and it motivated me on to work and achieve. I began to see that the things that had motivated my living to that point had all been so negative, and the trouble with negative motivation is that when you achieve what you are aiming for it is not worth having, nor do you dare count the cost of getting there. When I weighed under 8 stone it didn't mean a thing to me because I was so miserable, but now I can be 10 stone and live comfortably and happily with myself. When I had to pump myself full of amphetamines and laxatives to achieve a low weight, when I believed that being a size 10 was the only way to live, life was really not worth living.

I began to put together a programme aimed at helping people get out of the trap of compulsive eating. I based it on the sort of charts I had used to recognise my own bingeing habits, plus a sensible eating plan which would stabilise blood sugar levels, and constant monitoring and support to come to terms with and put right deep-seated personal problems.

The Maisner Centre was born, and I began to get my first clients. I saw them in the house I shared with Joe, and held meetings and workshops there. It was a large house with plenty of room for me to see clients and collect piles of books, cuttings and papers on the subject which now engrossed me, without getting in the way of Joe's work. Because he put a roof over my head in those early days of the Maisner Centre I was able to devote myself fully to my work. Boredom was a thing of the past. When I was not opening my post, sending off details of courses, or talking to clients, I would have my nose deep in a book, reading, reading all the time to learn more and more about my subject and all related aspects of it.

When Joe and I first met, our relationship was something that we both needed, but as we both progressed on our different paths our needs changed and the relationship ran out of steam. Joe worked long hours, at the office all day and writing in his study most of the night, and I was becoming absorbed in my courses and my new work with the Maisner Centre and growing further away from him each day.

The knowledge that we would eventually separate had been

somewhere in the distant back of my mind for some time. Although the actual conversation when we put our thoughts about splitting up into words was brief, the break-up did not happen overnight. It took months to reach the point where we realised we would part, and months more to actually get round to doing anything about it.

When I finally decided to talk to Joe about our relationship it was the television that brought it about. I had been giving a lot of thought to the influence that television has on people and so I decided to study Joe's viewing habits as a model for my research. When I got home he was as usual engrossed in some programme which did not interest me at all, and when I spoke to him he did not appear to notice I was in the room, much less hear what I was saying. I realised that this was a scene we had played over and over again; we were just not communicating, we had so little in common. I began to seriously question what we were doing trying to be a couple, and later that evening I marched into the study where he was working. 'I don't want to live with you any more' I said. 'I don't want to live with you,' he replied, and it was settled.

That television incident had just been the hair trigger that fired me into action. On its own it was no reason at all for ending a relationship, it just put a lot of other things into perspective. I had been aware for some time that I was caught in a trap of my own making with Joe; he needed someone around and I was emotionally dependent on him. To a large extent I was financially dependent as well. Without his money to back me I did not know how I would keep the Maisner Centre going. It was not enough to have a good idea, dedication and a belief that what I was doing was very necessary, I knew it would also have to be a businesslike and financially viable project to succeed. Without Joe to bail me out I went to the bank manager and asked for a loan of £500 to set myself up in an office. He turned me down. He could see no future in a business dealing with eating problems, and appeared to have little confidence in women in business. Then a former employer – a man – took up my case and talked the bank manager round. I got my money, even though I seethed with anger at the sexist way the deal had been done. I finally set up my offices at my new home in Hove.

I suppose my relationship with Joe had never really been right, even though I kept telling myself tomorrow would be better. Although I was unhappy I did not want to look at the idea of change because I could see no way out of the situation – or no way out that I believed I could cope with. From my limited viewpoint there seemed to be nothing beyond life with Joe – no job, no friends, nowhere to live, just a huge emptiness. In fact what I was looking at was a high wall which I had thrown up to protect myself from all the things I did not want to know about. Real life was on the other side of that wall but I could not even catch a glimpse of it until something dislodged the first brick to give me a view of what lay beyond.

People who are in the grip of depression live behind just such a wall, or maybe they see it as an impenetrable forest of tall dark trees. Whatever the image there seems no going forward, no way through, life stops after today.

Compulsive eaters, those caught up with drink, drugs or some other compulsion rooted in deep-seated personality problems, cannot see beyond the huge barriers they throw up in front of their faces. They lose the ability to think things through logically and plan for the future. How can you move forward when you cannot see what you are aiming for and don't even know if a future exists? It is very frightening, so the urge to remain safely tucked away behind the barriers is overwhelming. I continually come across people who find it impossible to see any reality in a different way of life, they are caught up in the dubious pay-offs of the present. Like Barry the alcoholic dying of drink, who does not really see what he has got to gain by giving up his drinking, he can't cope with life now and believes he could cope even less if he did not have the support of drink. The pain of coming off alcohol does not seem worth the effort, even if it might extend his life by a few years; a case of better the devil you know than the devil you don't.

Even Aunt Dolly, when she knew she was dying from lung disease, refused to give up smoking. Deep down I think she felt she had not much left to live for; the extra years did not seem worth the sacrifice of the comfort she got from her cigarettes. It was different for Brian, a man I met recently who had half a lung removed after developing lung cancer. Brian was much younger, had a family, work and a lot of things to live for so when he weighed up the balance it was worth keeping away from cigarettes and changing to a healthier life style.

It is easy enough for other people to step back and see the wider perspective, but when it is you that is cowering in the dark shadow of the wall it takes a lot of courage and determination to stand far enough away to see over the top and around. Worst of all is the belief that you can't break away, that you will never find a way through. You find months and years slipping by as you live half a life, afraid to face the challenge of going out to search for something better. More than once in my life I have lived with a man for the security of a roof over my head. It is hard to admit it but then I know thousands of other women are doing just the same thing, they cannot see any other way of surviving.

Mary lived with Peter for five years. He had a good job and she had a small child, no income and no self confidence. If she complained about anything he told her it was his house, if she didn't like it she could leave, knowing she had nowhere else to go. One day he walked out and left her. The house had been sold, and she ended up standing on the pavement holding her child's hand and surrounded by a suitcase and cardboard boxes which held all her worldly possessions. All the sacrifices had still not bought her any real security in the end. The experience of being abandoned had been heartbreaking, but later she was able to admit it was the best favour anyone ever did her. She vowed never to be dependent on anyone again, and worked and saved to build a home of her own which nobody could take away. She had been forced to knock down her protective wall and become a person in her own right, not just someone else's shadow.

If someone else does not come along with a sledgehammer and knock your wall down, the alternative is to dismantle it yourself brick by brick. As I look back over my life I can see that most of the major changes I made were of my own doing, they were decisions that had grown up from within myself. I would worry inwardly over a situation like a dog with a bone, gradually becoming aware that a change was needed but still putting up the 'I can'ts' that always held me back from immediate action: 'I can't get through the evening without a drink', 'I can't get up for work without a handful of pills', 'I can't pass the baker's shop without buying a bag of fresh scones', 'I can't carry on the Centre without Joe's help with the bills'. That phrase 'I can't' builds barriers, it stifles all possibilities and ambitions.

I see so many clients who have boxed themselves into a corner and forgotten the way out, and I can usually identify with every one of them. The circumstances may be different in each case but the emotion and attitude is the same. When you try to analyse the situation, usually the difficulty is that the change of lifestyle needed is drastic, and the person does not know how to carry out such radical changes, so does nothing at all. This is where I try to make my clients see that the way to tackle things is one small step at a time, like Patricia taking off her jacket. The aim is not a major new lifestyle overnight but a small step in the right direction, hopefully the first step of a long journey. Little changes can be just as important as big ones. When I split with Joe I had long black hair. One of the first things I did was visit the hairdresser for a new image with a short blonde style: I felt it helped me create the atmosphere of a whole new lifestyle, it was symbolic of the new me.

There is no advantage in deciding to make changes that swing too far to extremes, there is all the difference in the world between having ambition and having an obsession. Ambition is a positive driving force that can give shape and direction to your life, until you allow it to become obsessive, and then it turns like a savage dog and attacks you. One of the questions I ask my clients is what is their purpose in life, and it no longer surprises me to see some sort of negative reply written down. Things like 'I don't know', 'I want to weigh nine stone', or 'I can't see beyond my eating problem' crop up time and again, or other vague statements such as 'I want to be a good mother', or 'I want to make a nice home for my husband'. What do things like that mean? They are not real ambitions or dreams to motivate a better way of life. If you try to play fantasy games with people with compulsive problems you come across a desert, a blankness of vision for what lies beyond the next binge, the next drink, the next drug fix. These people are cocooned in their own little corner of existence and there is nothing out there, or nothing that is not too scary to look out and see. It is like living behind a wall with no-man's-land on the other side, so taking a risk, peering out and taking steps into the wilderness, is frightening. But it is very rewarding to discover that the land is, in reality, rich pasture full of real people, experiences, love and fulfilment.

After I climbed that first wall ten years ago and found out how worthwhile life can become, that empty wilderness that once seemed so huge has become a familiar garden, itself surrounded by a fence with new challenges beyond. I look forward to meeting those challenges now, they do not terrify me as the old ones did, and I think twice when I catch myself putting 'I can't' in the way of progress. It is not just myself, other people often try to shoot me down when I suggest trying anything new. But when people say to me 'You can't do that', I look at their lives and see what they are really saying is 'I can't do that, so why should you'? Too many years can be wasted believing what other people say you should or should not be doing.

For example, one of my clients used to be a headmistress but she hated the job, and that frustration and basic unhappiness was at the root of many problems, including compulsive eating. When she began to look at her life she decided to give in her notice at the school, and then she announced her new job was as a cleaner. It caused shock waves all round, everyone tried to talk her out of it, her family were horrified at the way she appeared to be throwing away the career and respectability she had built up. Her mother in particular was very difficult, she had enjoyed the prestige of introducing her daughter the headmistress and could not think of people meeting her daughter the char. It hurt her pride too much. But my client carried on and before long had built up a thriving little cleaning business which brought her a lot of satisfaction and pride. Her self-esteem was boosted and many of her problems disappeared.

For some time I have been a keen Scrabble player. I took it up originally because I found it distracted me from eating, and now it has become something that stimulates my mind and does wonders for increasing my vocabulary. Recently I have thought about joining the local Scrabble Club, and that little niggling voice inside tries to tell me not to be so ridiculous, I am not nearly good enough a player. But another voice says why shouldn't I, if it is something that would give me pleasure and introduce me to new people, what does it matter if I am not very good? In every contest somebody always has to be the one to come last. If I really want to join the Scrabble Club I will disregard the excuses I am making to myself and go along to find out if I would really enjoy being a member. I need to take the risk of that first step, disregarding my fear of being made to look stupid and ignorant.

One achievement of which I am particularly proud is the magazine I shall be launching in the spring. For a long time I had been mulling over the idea of a magazine aimed at people with eating disorders, but there seemed to be so many barriers in my way. People kept telling me it wouldn't work, I couldn't keep on producing the issues, and where would I get the finance?

Gradually, though, I battered down all the barriers and proved everybody wrong. I knew I would never raise the money if I didn't ask for it –so I asked – and I got it! A lot of my spare time is now spent on working to produce the first issue and arrange material for subsequent ones.

I proved to myself, and to everybody else, that I could meet that challenge and overcome it.

If I have not achieved something positive during each day, however small a thing it may be, I feel that day has not been used to the full. What a huge leap forward from the time when, like so many others, my only ambition was to survive through another day! Just going through the motions of living is a waste of life when there is so much going on in the world, but until you try doing things you don't know what you are missing. I am always thinking of one of the people who used to work for me at the Maisner Centre, who was forever barking down the telephone at clients in her high-pitched voice, 'Life is not a rehearsal!'

There is more to life than the constant search for a slim figure. I accept that people do feel more confident when they are slim, or rather when they believe they look good, and I cannot imagine anything worse that being really fat again, but what happens with compulsive eaters and bulimics is that they only get slim when things are going well for them and their self confidence is boosted. Inevitably that exciting new job gets boring, the wonderful love affair ends, and they go back to bingeing and put on weight because they have not built up inner resources to fall back on. When I was a size 10 I could no more stand up and give a talk to a room full of people than fly to the moon, but I can take on the challenge of doing that now. At last I understand that the size of my dress is irrelevant, it is the quality of what I have to say that will hold my audience, they will be listening to my lecture, not criticising how I look. What is the point of trying to give a lecture if you have 32" hips but nothing to say? The real priorities of life are the substantial, lasting things. So many times people say to me that they believe all their problems will go away when they are slim; I ask them if they have ever been slim before, and usually they have, time and time again, but it always went wrong – their problems had not gone away.

I have so many good ambitions but it is at that final step of actually putting them into practice that I so often fall down. Like most other people I can persuade myself of a million reasons why I should be doing something and then I still don't do it. One way I find of motivating me to actually go somewhere and do something is to make a contract with somebody else. For example, I love my Aerobics in Water classes at the nearby swimming pool; when I am there I thoroughly enjoy myself, and feel wonderful afterwards. But there is always some very good reason why I shouldn't go – I'm too busy, it's too cold, etc., etc.

Because I arrange to meet another person and we go together, I have to make the effort to get out of the hourse, and I never regret it.

I keep asking people what this elusive thing called motivation is: why do some people appear to possess it in generous quantities while others find it impossible to grasp? I have not yet come up with a clear cut definition, mainly I think because motivation is something that means different things to different people. One area which should not be ignored when considering why some people are more self motivated than others is to do with early training in attitude to life. Children who are encouraged to explore and learn and try things for themselves from an early age, without being put down when they fail or being held back by the fears or prejudices of the grown ups who surround them, are more likely to carry on trying and looking positively forward throughout their life.

I think the story Mary told me about her early ambitions to play the piano is a good illustration of this. At the age of seven she badgered her parents to let her have piano lessons. Eventually they agreed and bought a piano which was an elegant piece of furniture chosen to look nice in the corner of the living room. Mary continued her weekly lessons for several years and passed quite a few exams but never received any support or encouragement from her parents. She was not allowed to practise when her father was at home because he did not like the noise; her parents never asked her to play to them or came to listen when she had mastered a tune, her music was something which she had to work at alone with the doors shut and the implied suggestion that she was annoying the rest of the family. In the end she gave up playing, just as she gave up many other interests because she never received any positive response from her parents towards what she was doing. When I met her as a grown up she faced problems in motivating herself to take up any interests or hobbies.

The other day I was in a self-service cafeteria queueing up behind a mother and her small son. He asked for an orange juice and when it was passed over to him he managed to knock it over, spilling most of the contents of the glass in the tray. The mother, was annoyed, calling him stupid and clumsy. I wondered how many times a day the child was given that message by his mother every day with enough repetition he would come to believe it and always think of himself as stupid, lacking the ability to break out of the mould and prove himself something better. How many times was I told as a child that I mumbled, I stood badly, I was fat. My father constantly tried to improve me but only succeeded in giving me a hopelessly bad image of myself which has followed me most of my life.

I find some of my clients so frustrating, I get tempted to give up on them completely, because they just do not seem to have any real desire to get better. They are constantly telling me how desperately they want to get their eating under control, but they never actually do any of the things which I suggest will help them. Louella is a typical case. She has a good job, plenty of money, and a nice home, but she is utterly bored and her life is empty. She never goes anywhere or meets anyone, she sits at home with her husband every evening and follows him to watch him play football every weekend without any ambition to have an interest or hobby of her own. I feel I have totally failed to get through to her the need to boost her self-esteem by being a person in her own right, contributing something positive to the world and building a fulfilled life of her own. That is the only way she will realistically be able to come to terms with her eating problems, but there is no glimmer of motivation to set the process in motion.

It took me half a lifetime to painfully realise you don't overcome boredom and lack of self-esteem by waiting for someone else to hand you the magic cure on a plate. There must have been many opportunities during those years when I was in the elevator going down when I could have changed direction, but I didn't take any of them, I didn't even see them as I was too locked in my own little world. Motivation must owe a lot to timing; when the right set of circumstances meets the right frame of mind the push comes along to get you moving back up the staircase to a better life in the real world.

HALF FULL
OR HALF EMPTY?

The first day I moved into my new offices it snowed. As I stamped my feet on the doormat and turned the key – my key – in the lock – my lock – I felt ready to get going with my new life. With £500 wheedled out of the grudging bank, a filing cabinet, a typewriter and all the paraphernalia of office business surrounding me, I sat behind my desk and waited with an inner surge of excitement for something to happen.

Half an hour later the ceiling collapsed. The weight of snow on the old, leaking roof had found a weak spot and a watery blizzard of snow and plaster cascaded over the carpet. As I collected brooms and buckets to start clearing up I couldn't help mocking myself rather cynically: so much for happy ever after!

You could say I am not one of those people blessed with good luck, but then I don't believe in luck. You make your own good or bad fortune and when things go wrong there is always some lesson to be learned from the experience, no matter how miserable or shattering it may be at the time. Learning from our mistakes is the most positive way of coming to terms with all the things that go wrong over a lifetime. There is no way I could have assembled my philosophy of life and put it into practice if I had had an easy time and sat back at my ease to dream up theories. All the advice I am able to give to my clients is the result of experience in the field. Whatever mistakes they make and problems they bring on themselves, the chances are I have been there before them and so I can relate exactly to the way they are feeling. The only difference is that I have had time to struggle through the quagmire they are at present caught up in, I have at long last learnt the hard way how to get problems under control, while my clients still have a lot of learning to do. I can usually recognise those who are prepared to make the necessary changes needed to catch me up and even overtake me; these are the ones who will in time get their life and eating under control.

With each new client I explain that a journey lies ahead of them if they want to get from where they are at the moment, point A, to where they would like to be, point B. That journey will mean making changes and they have to face up to this and accept it before they set out if they hope to reach their destination. Time and again I meet with a totally negative response, they are not even prepared to consider making changes. That is not always the end of the story; sometimes once they begin on the Maisner Course that attitude changes, but some never really start out from base. I try to encourage each client to progress at his or her own pace. Some make remarkably rapid advances, others take a long time to get started but arrive in the end, others wallow around for months and years and never really get anywhere. It is quite common for people to play at getting started – they say they are making changes but in fact they are just carrying on in the same old habits. Then one day they suddenly decide to stop playing and take the whole thing seriously, sometimes they even phone me up and say 'Right, I'm ready to get my eating under control now'.

Leslie was one of those, and she sticks in my mind as being one of my more dramatic clients. She had been coming to me on and off for a long time, sometimes making a bit of progress and then sinking back into terrible fits of black depression, bingeing and thoughts of suicide. One evening a friend who knows Leslie rang my doorbell in a state of great anxiety: he had just driven past Leslie's home and seen an ambulance parked outside, doors open and blue light flashing. He pulled over and leaped out of his car just as Leslie was carried out on a stretcher, unconscious and looking deathly pale. We telephoned the hospital but got no details, not being relatives we were not entitled to information, even though Leslie is quite alone in the world and we are probably the nearest she has to anyone who cares about her. Eventually we discovered what had happened. In a fit of depression she had got a pair of steel knitting needles and stuck them into an electric socket in an attempt to kill herself. She recovered, but her hands were badly burned and will probably be scarred for life.

In time she came round to see me again, saying this time she really wanted to change, she wanted to get her life and her eating under control and she was prepared to accept that she could not go on and on in the same old ways. I told her straight that if she really meant what she said about making changes she would have to make a start right away, and the first thing to do was to enrol for a self-esteem workshop. I saw the shutters come down, that evasive look came into her eyes as she cast about like a trapped animal for an easy way out. 'I can't go to a workshop,' she blurted out, 'I'm much too shy'. I felt exasperated. 'Why do you think they have these courses?' I asked her. 'They are designed for people who think they are too shy to cope with life. People would not need to go if they already had enough self-esteem'.

Reluctantly Leslie agreed to go. I also suggested she go along to the drug abuse clinic, where she would find a friendly supportive crowd who would understand how she felt. She said she was too shy to go to this either, but eventually agreed provided I would find someone to go along with her to the first meeting. I sent Richard, a young man I knew from the drug abuse centre, to walk with her. It proved unexpectedly successful, the two of them hit it off together and Leslie was prepared to talk a little to him and listen to what he had to say. He admitted to her that he had been bulimic, something he had never even mentioned to me, although I was well aware of his drug problem. That goes to show the stigma of bulimia can be even greater than that of drug addiction. Since then Leslie has made no more suicide attempts and is greatly improved in self-esteem. Much to my surprise she is shaking off the huge load of inhibitions under which she has struggled all her life. I never stop believing in miracles.

I have learnt how important it is to recognise our own limitations and adjust our lifestyle and expectations accordingly. For example, while I have no problems with one-to-one relationships I still find large groups and parties more difficult than I would like. Nowadays I just don't put myself through that kind of ordeal unless it is important, I know I find it stressful and it takes a lot out of me so I prefer to direct my energies into things which I know I do well and I enjoy. But that does not mean that now and again I don't push myself to do things that I really want to, testing my abilities to handle situations I think I might not be able to cope with. Sometimes I find I cope better than I expected and even find myself enjoying the situation.

I don't push myself merely because other people say I should, though. I will only do it if the motivation is there inside me. For example, I recently had to face the daunting prospect of giving a talk on eating disorders to an audience of 160 professional medical people. I was absolutely terrified, but I knew it was something I really wanted to do, so I pushed myself – and the supreme sense of achievement I felt when I'd done it made all the panic and nerves worthwhile!

I try to get the idea of realistic goals across to all my clients who are running to the comfort of food because they feel they have to push themselves to confront situations and perform duties to which they are just not suited. This usually includes those who are in the wrong job because it is what others expect of them, or the wrong marriage because it is what they expect of themselves.

Joanna is a typical example, she owned a big house in Brighton and flogged up and down to her high-pressure job in the City every day. By the time she got home at night she was exhausted and the weekends were just a time to recover and do a bit of housework before Monday morning. All she found time for was bingeing, everything else was focused on surviving through her working day. She had got herself into the trap of buying a house with a huge mortgage that could only be supported by staying on in her high-paid London job, and she was so caught up in the treadmill of work and money she had become too exhausted to find a way out. The first time I suggested perhaps she sell her house and get something smaller and cheaper the idea barely registered; paying the mortgage had become an accepted part of her existence, she only looked to me to sort out her problems with food, not with money. But in time she did become able to reassess her whole life, to take a step back and see that if she was miserable, bingeing, and the quality of her life was rock bottom, owning a big house was no compensation. It took a long time before she realised for herself that she had committed herself to something more than she could successfully cope with, but even then it was not easy to come to terms with making changes without feeling she had failed.

As with many such cases, it was only after Joanna had sold her house, given up her job, and settled for a way of life that did not put such an intolerable burden on her that she fully realised the wisdom of the changes. She found herself going out in the evenings, making friends, taking up new interests in a way she had not believed possible before, and of course she was no longer bingeing through sheer exhaustion and stress. Her whole lifestyle was so vastly improved she did not miss her expensive house, and settled happily into a one-bedroom flat. Joanna was fortunate because she was able to see the positive advantages of her new life and did not punish herself with feelings of failure and guilt. It is an easy but pointless exercise to step out of one negative situation only to replace it with another.

When I first started up the Maisner Centre I was doing the courses for next to nothing and I just did not get the right sort of commitment from my clients. It is important for people to pay in order to feel they are receiving something worthwhile in return. When people say they can't afford my fees the first question I usually ask them is how much they are spending on food: anyone with a compulsive eating problem is likely to be running up huge grocery bills. It helps to put the cost of the fees in perspective.

When I was in the grip of my eating, drinking and drugs problems I did not really worry in the same way about things. I panicked about how I would survive until tomorrow, but I floated on a cloud above many of life's more mundane problems. Someone who is totally wrapped up in diets, calories and reaching 8 stone 5 is not really interested in what is going on in the world, it is a form of escapism. If war breaks out in some remote country or a child is murdered in a distant town it doesn't matter, it doesn't even penetrate into a mind totally turned in on itself. When you are a bulimic all the jagged edges are taken off life because you are too obsessed with eating and vomiting to notice them. It can come as a shock when you start to get better and come out of your self-centred state to find the world is far from perfect, that all those jagged edges are still there ready to tear you apart. Realising that life is far from ideal is a difficult adjustment to make, but it is a change of attitude that is vital for everyone on the road to recovery.

When I was surviving through the day to my next drink I never dreamed I would spend hours worrying over getting my VAT returns right, discussing if I should vote in local elections, or being moved to tears by a story of cruelty to children in the newspaper. I suppose I worry just as much now as I did when I was obsessed with my weight, but now I worry about things outside myself, in other words I have rejoined the human race.

An obsessive illness can cut you off from reality so totally that when you get better you wonder how you could ever have got your head so deeply buried in the sand. One of my clients recently told me she had been to hospital for a scan of the ovaries because she had not had a period for months. I asked her if she had told the doctor she was bulimic and made herself sick six times a day, but she had not mentioned it, she had not even associated her bulimia with her menstrual problems. That reminds me very much of myself at the height of my laxative addiction. I went to the doctor about my haemorrhoids, I was concerned because I was losing so much blood, but never associated it with the vast amount of laxatives I was swallowing. I have lost count of the times I convinced myself I must have cancer, mainly because I just could not see any future for myself, life seemed to stop dead not very far ahead.

I find it very encouraging that at last the medical profession is beginning to acknowledge the existence of eating problems. However, quite often when I talk to doctors, even experienced specialists, they say they rarely see patients with severe eating problems. They are quite shocked when I tell them they probably see several hundred a year but just do not recognise them; compulsive eaters and bulimics are very adept at covering their tracks. Too many people, even doctors, assume that compulsive eaters are fat and bulimics are thin. Sometimes this is so, but at other times the reverse may apply. A lot of compulsive eaters are thin because they diet strenuously or fast for long periods, then they binge. When you add up their calorie intake over a week it is actually less than their needs, particularly if they use up a lot of calories by exercise or in their work. Bulimics are often overweight because a lot of calories are absorbed before they throw up, very few throw up everything they have eaten or every time they eat, so if they eat a lot they will put on weight. With laxatives most of the calories are absorbed before the laxatives start to work. Diuretic takers are only losing water and minerals, they are not losing calories at all.

Whatever the size and shape the outsider may observe, it will bear little resemblance to the image that person has of their own body. Almost all compulsive eaters and bulimics see themselves as fat and long to be thinner, whether they weigh 18 stone or 7 stone. Some bulimics purge for a lot of other reasons, such as to punish themselves and other people and to relieve themselves of stress and negative feelings. The doctor is not helped in making his diagnosis by the fact that often even the patient herself does not fully appreciate that she has an eating problem; total obsession with eating, dieting and bingeing has become such a way of life she cannot imagine a life without these things.

The biggest binge of my life occurred when I had more or less got my eating under control, at the time of my early relationship with Joe. It all began with the wardrobe of course, that wardrobe I wanted Joe to buy me to hang my new clothes in. I just would not let the subject drop even while we were out doing our week's shopping at the supermarket. By the time we got home that day I was angry. I marched indoors while Joe unloaded the shopping in the hall and went off to park the car. Parking was a problem in that district and by the time he had got rid of the car and walked home it was some 40 minutes later and I had binged my way through what I later calculated to be 14,000 calories worth of food, a good proportion of our week's groceries. Joe found me flat out on the bed, groaning that I must have picked up a stomach bug, I felt so ill. He never noticed the shopping was missing. It was a tin of biscuits on top of my angry state that had set me off. I started with four biscuits, then I went back for six, then ten, then the rest of the tin. After that I started in on the remainder of the shopping, and once started there was no going back. Turning out baskets and carrier bags, ripping open packets and boxes, I stuffed myself until I felt sick and unable to move. I don't think I had ever crammed so much food down in one go before, but it was as if this was some kind of final fling. From that day on I have never had a large binge again.

Starting up the Maisner Centre gave me a new purpose in life. Like so many of my clients, I have never been the sort of person who does things by halves. If I am going to drink I drink a lot; if I make a mess of my life it has to be a total disaster, so when I started to make changes and get better it was inevitable that step by step I would go all the way to a new lifestyle, ending up a leading expert in my subject. The trouble is that so many of my clients think that one day I was hiding away at home bingeing and boozing and the next, as if by some divine miracle, I was running the Maisner Centre, in control of my life and helping thousands of others to sort out their problems. It just wasn't like that. In between was a lot of struggling and misery and failure. Perhaps if I knew how to do things in moderation I might have saved myself a lot of those heartaches.

I caught a glimpse of this attitude in someone at the drug abuse centre recently. I had a headache and asked her if she happened to have an Aspirin. She dived into a huge handbag and pulled out a tube from which she shook about ten tablets into my hand.

'I only need two, thanks,' I said, thinking she had made a mistake. 'No take them all, ten will do you much more good,' she replied. That was her whole attitude to life, totally over the top. No wonder she had problems.

Even when you climb back up and life is under control that is never quite the end of the story. Even those who are completely cured will suffer ups and downs in the normal course of their everyday life, and someone like me can never expect to completely shake off every one of the skeletons that have rattled around over the years. The most we can expect is to keep them neatly stored away in the very back of the cupboard and keep a constant vigil so we never let the cupboard doors swing too wide open.

It came as quite a shock to me to realise a few years ago that although I had turned the corner and completely changed the course of my life it was not all sunshine and roses, and I had allowed myself to slip into another negative phase. It was as if when nobody was looking I had sneaked back into that elevator and lowered myself down a few floors. Probably none of my clients, or even those who knew me quite well, realised what a state I was in; I have got quite cunning at hiding my worst problems over the years. Worst of all I didn't realise it myself for quite some time, then it came home to me that I might think I had put the past behind me but I was still vulnerable to all my old weaknesses, if I let myself slide. I did see clearly then that I again had a choice before me: either I could let it all go and sink back into the twilight world of misery which would totally engulf me, or I could make one last effort to climb my way back up once and for all.

It was a combination of events that set me back off on the downward plunge. The Maisner Centre was progressing in its usual fashion of personal success and financial crisis, my work was becoming recognised and I had two books published, so I was not dissatisfied with what I had achieved. Then my tax affairs started to go wrong. Due to my ignorance of the tax laws and the fact that I had lived abroad for so many years, I assumed you only had to be assessed for income tax if you had an income. As I was not earning a living out of the Maisner Centre I did not bother to fill in tax returns. I was also unfortunate in putting my trust in an accountant who turned out to be negligent, and the whole thing turned into a nightmare. I was bombarded with huge demands for money which I did not owe, and was threatened with court proceedings and bankruptcy. However much I argued and fought I could not seem to sort it out. The worry nagged at me continually and gave me no rest, I could see horrible visions of everything I had built up being ripped away from me, I would lose my home, my work and my growing reputation as an expert in eating disorders. Thoughts of loss and ruin poisoned my days and tortured my nights so I became edgy, tired and short tempered, there was little pleasure in working on new projects when in the back of my mind was the fear it might all be for nothing.

In the end I went to the doctor because I was hardly sleeping at all and he prescribed some tablets to help me repair my shattered nerves and get some rest. I began taking them and for a while felt grateful for the margin of release from tension they gave me. The sharp edge of my panic and urge to do something about an impossible situation was temporarily blunted. But around the same time I started having trouble with my teeth; as if things were not bad enough I paced about my flat in the early hours of the morning with agonising toothache night after night. Eventually the dentist broke the news that there was nothing more he could do to save my front teeth, they would have to come out. I was shattered. I have always had good teeth. Even in the bad old days when I felt disgusted by my body I still held onto a pride in my nice teeth. Now with my vastly improved self image I valued them even more. As I studied them for the last time in my dressing table mirror a kind of despair overwhelmed me. Losing my teeth seemed a blow more distressing then I could bear.

But the operation went ahead and when it was all over I was in a state of weakness and depression. My lovely front teeth were gone for ever, I was an old lady with false teeth, my body was falling apart and my finances were crumbling, what was there left for me to keep struggling on for? That night I woke up feeling alarmingly ill. I contacted the emergency doctor, whose verdict was that I had suffered some form of allergic reaction to the antibiotics given after the extraction of my teeth. Looking back on the whole episode I would not be surprised if it was a panic attack that completely overwhelmed me in my time of extreme crisis.

When I recovered I had to face the long, weary drag back to health. For a long time I never went out of the house, I could not face people, I just wanted to hide away with my misery.

Fortunately it was at this stage that I met Vic. Vic was someone I admired and respected for his very real qualities. I owe a lot to him, he helped me survive a very grim period of my life. He would come breezing in through my front door, making fun of me and ignoring the fact that I was bad tempered and grouched that I just wanted to be left alone. He would pace up and down pretending to tear his hair out and whining, 'I can't work today, I've lost all my teeth' in a comic parody of me at my worst. It annoyed me, but it reached me and chased me out of the fearful downward spiral. It taught me to see the funny side of things! I was able to look at myself critically at last and see the state I had slipped into, there was no excitement in my life, no challenge, no spark, just misery and fear and bleakness, nothing held any joy for me. Joy is something we recognise when we experience it but cannot even imagine when we are in the grim shadows of depression.

I thought of myself at my lowest ebb just the other day when I went into the living room one morning and discovered my prayer plant in bloom. The flower brought me a rush of supreme happiness, I drove my visitors mad all day ushering them in to admire the precious bloom, totally caught up in the thrill of this litle miracle. That was the feeling that was missing when I let myself slide downwards, it was the element I lacked through so much of my early life when I did not know how to look up and see happiness, I always kept my eyes fixed downwards on the bare ground and travelled downwards on the elevator of life'.

One of the conclusions I came to early on was that the tablets I was still taking on the doctor's prescription were merely numbing my reason and letting me hide away from reality in the kind of fog. I needed to be realistic and sort out my problems one way or another, not hide away from them, so I stopped taking the tablets.

Recently there has been a lot more awareness about the problems of Ativan, the drug I was on, its addictive properties and the problems of withdrawal. When I stopped taking them I felt dreadful, quite spaced out a lot of the time and seized by horrifying fits of shaking. In search of help I went along to a drug group meeting and found myself in the company of drug addicts and alcoholics, most of whom were in a far worse state than myself. Attending that group helped me a lot; in fact I still pay visits from time to time because I find there such a rich seam of life, I hear so many gripping and often heartbreaking stories, and yet there is more humour there than anywhere else I go. It is a constant source of inspiration to me in my continual inquisitive searchings about people and their compulsions.

I began to realise, as I sat through fascinating evenings of human revelations from people hooked on alcohol or drugs or both, that these people have a tremendous amount in common with compulsive eaters. They suffer all the same basic problems of low self-esteem and negative thinking, they are hiding in their compulsion instead of meeting the problems of life head on. What a person chooses to become addicted to is largely irrelevant: food, alcohol, work, exercise, it's all one and the same because an addict's problem is himself.

When I could once again see clearly how I was throwing everything away by giving in to the negative feelings of misery and despair, I began to look for ways of pulling myself back up. People had been telling me not to worry about my finances, that I could get a second mortgage and borrow the money I needed to pay off the Inland Revenue. But I wouldn't listen, I was convinced I could not do it, and all the time I was giving in to that negative state. Now I began to feel positive again I found the energy to look into solutions and did in fact re-mortgage to sort out my financial problems.

Nobody has ever come up with a valid reason why some people are able to see life in a positive way and others only view the negative. We are all handed a telescope to view the world: is it just a matter of luck which end we happen to place up to our eye? I was talking to a medical friend recently who was called to visit a man dying from cancer. She went prepared for a sombre session, hoping at best to relieve some of the terrible pain he was suffering, and escape without becoming too drained herself. She came away nearly three hours later saying she had not laughed so much in a long time. Here was a huge spirit trapped in a broken-down body. He had already fought off two bouts of cancer and was still involved in creative work and full of anecdotes about his adventurous life. My friend had become used to dealing with fear and negativity from patients with far less serious complaints and found this man a joy to treat and a privilege to meet.

That conversation reminded me of a man I met one day at the yacht club, who was hopping around on crutches and who told me he was due to have his foot amputated later that week. Because of his bright and breezy attitude I did not take him seriously, but he was telling the truth, and when I went to visit him in hospital a couple of weeks later I learnt they had removed not only the foot but a large part of the leg as well. It was all the result of an accident, and there he was sitting up in bed surrounded by papers and legal books, making a whole new career out of how he was going to sue for compensation. In the next bed was a man who had also had a leg amputated three weeks before. He lay with his face to the wall, crying. He had no reserves of spirit to help him come to terms with a new and different life without his leg. I didn't even try to speak to him, I just couldn't think of anything to say. But I did wonder, and I still do, how two men side by side in hospital beds could respond so differently to the same disaster.

So often, negative thinking is little more than illusion. We build scenarios in our heads and convince ourselves that the problems we see are all there is to life. When you crawl out of bed on a bad morning, groaning at the prospect of struggling through another day, the world is exactly the same place as it was on that morning when you woke up, the sun was shining, and you felt a pleasant anticipation about the hours ahead. All that has changed is your way of perceiving things. I will never forget the very first time I was interviewed for a national magazine. I didn't sleep a wink the night before, I was so frantic about what questions the reporter would ask me, how she would interpret my answers, what it would be like to expose myself in print to thousands of strangers. I was outwardly calm but inwardly reeling when the journalist arrived, and to make things worse she walked in looking cool, calm and collected and breezed through the interview with supreme confidence. I later got to know her quite well. Imagine how we laughed when I discovered it was actually her first interview as well. She too had suffered a sleepless night at the thought of having to tackle this worldly wise woman, and was overawed by my show of confidence.

What a pair of idiots we were, screwing ourselves up to meet a totally imagined challenge.

Where things go so badly wrong in our lives is when we back out of a situation without even facing it because we have convinced ourselves we cannot cope. Several times that morning I had been on the point of picking up the telephone and cancelling the interview, and yet that article led on to a lot of other things in my life, and was crucially important. The compulsive eater binges instead of taking up a challenge, the alcoholic has a few drinks, it is all one and the same; it is escapism.

But when the urge to cut and run comes over you, how do you find a more positive approach? It might be easier to draw up guidelines if everyone reacted in the same sort of way to similar situations, but what one person will take in their stride completely freaks another out, and vice versa. Myself for example – I go into internal panic in a crowd and bloom in one-to-one conversations, but Joe was exactly the opposite. I have seen him stand up and give an excellent speech at a grand banquet, or lecture to a large audience, completely confident and in control. And yet if he had an appointment with the doctor he would be fussing about the house, fretting over clean socks and asking me what I thought he should say.

One of my clients is the managing director of a large company. She got in touch with me because she weighed 18 stone and thought my eating plan might help her lose weight. She appeared self confident to me at the initial interview, and I could see why she had done so well in business. I introduced her to the Maisner Method and explained how it meant analysing her eating patterns and altering those things in her life which were causing her to binge. The next time I spoke to her she had lost a stone in weight and she told me she now had the confidence to believe she could lose weight because she had actually achieved something. I was astounded that a woman who appeared outwardly to be so confident and such a high achiever actually had this personal weak spot. In her mind she could see herself subduing a board of directors but she could not see herself as slim. As I worked more on this case I began to see how this attitude was reflected in her personal relationships. At work she was giving off positive energy, motivating her staff and handling problems with confidence, so she was getting a similar sort of response from those she did business with. At home she lacked confidence in herself as a person away from the office desk, she could not project herself positively to others on a personal level and so she found relationships difficult. It was almost as if she had found a way to survive by being two separate people, the business woman was a mask she put on when she walked in at her office door.

In many ways I play the same trick. I can laze around at home just relaxing, but when I have a client coming I get myself together and play the role of efficient counsellor. I cannot hope to get positive results from people if I am projecting a negative state on to them, and even when I was at my lowest I was aware of this and always did my best to put on my positive working overcoat. When I go to the drug group it still surprises me a bit to see how 'normal' the people there seem to be. They are all there because inside they have terrible problems they can't handle, but each one is putting on his positive 'I can cope' face to the world. But there is one girl who comes who does not bother with such things. She turns up late looking scruffy and dirty, she makes no attempt to please anyone, is rude and angry, and the whole room picks up these vibrations. It is interesting to observe how people respond to her: the humour and words of wisdom are still there but there is an extra crackle to the atmosphere. This girl believes everyone hates her, so she is only prepared to receive negative emotions from everyone she meets. It is as if each person she confronts is a mirror reflecting back the anger she is herself giving off.

In recent years I have tried to cut myself off from negative people in my personal life. I realise I just pick up bits of their negativity, whereas when I am with people who are positive and vital I begin to spark with an enthusiasm of my own. Perpetual moaners really drag me down, so I ask myself whether I really need them in my life. We are surrounded by so much doom and gloom on the television and in the newspapers it is no wonder so many people feel depressed about the state of the world, and yet there are so many good things going on which never get reported. I realise now the importance of searching out the positive side of every event and I always try to encourage my clients to do the same.

I think one of the most positive influences in my life, if not the most positive of all, has been my son Peter. I can't say if things would have been much different if he had never been born, but I do know that I have always loved him deeply and needed him in my life. It surprised me a little that he should have grown up into such an ordinary, sensible sort of person, considering the rather bizarre circumstances he sometimes found me leading him into during his childhood. I believe he survived largely unscathed because I loved him so much. When I compare his childhood to my own I know which I believe to be a better preparation for life.

Nowadays he is a married man and a father, and the latest in a long line of happy things he has brought me is my little granddaughter. Being a grandmother must be the great compensation for growing older!

My parents, in contrast, were a negative influence on me. I know I still let my father get to me, but he no longer has the power to really put me down in the way he cramped my personality when I was a child. Perhaps that is another of the benefits of growing older.

I still come across clients time and again who are totally under the sway of their families and it causes so much frustration and pent-up anger that I am not surprised they turn to bingeing in secret. Lorna was a teacher who handled her work well and got through life quite adequately during term time. Then the holidays would arrive and her family packed her off to look after her elderly grandmother. Granny was a miserable old tyrant who ran Lorna off her feet, the holidays were something to dread and after a few days Lorna would be sneaking off to the kitchen and the comfort of food. She didn't want to spend all her free time chained to this awful old woman but she had no idea how to escape, could not begin to tell her family she was not prepared to do it any more. I told her my belief that we owe our existence to our parents, not our life, and she agreed; then we talked over ways in which she could negotiate to meet them half way over the situation. It was another case where there was an obvious social and emotional pressure leading directly to bingeing. All the diets and slimming foods in the world would not cure Lorna's weight problem while she was eating to comfort herself.

Usually the trouble with such situations is that so much emotional involvement is tied up with the problem that, if there is a logical solution, it becomes invisible in the tangle of negative responses. When it is me that has a problem I get out a pencil and paper – usually in the small hours of the morning which is my time of greatest inspiration – and write down the positives and negatives of a situation. That was how I eventually managed to convince myself that people do actually survive and live normal happy lives without their front teeth. It was a plan I used with Lorna, getting her to write down all aspects of the situation so she could view it more clearly. Writing things down is often a way of picking out the facts of a case from the assumptions. We are all so influenced by our own negative trains of thought we just slip into the same old responses without challenging them and so get stuck in the same old ruts.

When I was with the drug group one evening, Jeff, a homosexual, was complaining about the way the man he lived with treated him. 'He knows he makes me angry when he goes to visit his brother,' he said. 'How do you know he knows this?' one of the others challenged; 'Have you told him it makes you angry?' another added. In self-help groups such as this, where everyone is suffering from the same sort of problems, it is sometimes possible to bring misconceptions to light. Jeff got annoyed and the subject was dropped, but I mulled the idea over and the next time I saw Lorna I asked her straight out if she had ever told her family how much she hated being sent to look after her grandmother.

'They know it makes me unhappy,' she said. 'Do they really know?' I insisted. 'Are you sure they understand how much it is affecting you?' She went away and thought it over for a while, then she tackled her mother and told her a few home truths. The conversation surprised her. Because she had always dutifully gone off to grandmother's every holiday her mother had never really taken her half-hearted grumbling seriously, she had never fully appreciated how much Lorna's life was being overshadowed. It was the basis of negotiations for the future.

I have a trait in my nature which has at times got me into difficulties, but which I now see and use as a positive tool. Whenever someone tells me I can't do something it becomes very important to me to do it and prove them wrong. When I was young my grandmother used to tell me that fat women never got married, which was probably one of the reasons why I rushed off and married the first man I met. I just had to show her that this fat person could get a husband. When I worked at a garage the men would never take my longing to get behind the wheel seriously, they took it for granted that women don't race fast cars. How I showed them as I scorched around the track at Brand's Hatch! It's strange but nowadays I don't even own a car and never drive, perhaps because there is nobody now telling me I can't do it.

I haven't changed my basic nature, I doubt that anyone can do that, but I have learnt to see myself from a different viewpoint. The obstinacy that got me into so much trouble when I was younger is the same characteristic of my nature that won't let me go completely under when times get tough–it has both its negative and its positive traits. It has now become a way of life to me to ride out the everyday problems which once would have thrown me completely for days. Sometimes whole batches of my post go missing; there I am sitting in my office, paying my staff, and no work is delivered for us to get on with. It makes me mad when I telephone the Post Office and get excuses like 'The new postman doesn't know his way to the sorting office', but I don't go off and binge or lock up the office and disappear for a week; I rant around, punch a few innocent cushions, and wait until the next delivery. Nobody's life is one long high, although I think I once expected mine should be and I was somehow a failure if I suffered a bad patch. One thing about coming out of the shadows is that you learn to see things in a longer perspective. I now know my post will arrive eventually, the rain will stop pouring down and the sun will shine in due course, and pleasant surprises and enjoyable experiences are waiting for me somewhere around the corner.

The other day I had three telephone calls on the trot from people who complained the Maisner Method wasn't working, they were not losing weight, they were not getting their eating under control. My period was due, and I was feeling bloated and short tempered. I began seriously asking myself why I was bothering, why try to help all these people who were just too negatively motivated to begin to help themselves. Then my daughter-in-law called to say the baby had given her first proper smile, an unexpected cheque arrived by the second post, together with a letter from a long-standing client saying at long last she had managed to sort out her marriage problems and she was feeling happy and confident for the first time in years. By the evening I had to admit the world wasn't such a bad place and the Maisner Centre was needed and doing a worthwhile job. I treated myself to my favourite late night snack because I know I always get extra hungry at pre-menstrual times, and went to bed content and satisfied with my life. I had survived a day which had started out really badly, and to me that is important. I can ride the ups and downs instead of letting the first dip set me on a downhill path that just gathers speed and momentum until I crash into disaster.

In the days when I spent long evenings sitting in Spanish bars I would stare at the glass in front of me and grumble that it was half empty. Nowadays as I am talking on the telephone to a client I reach out for my cup of coffee and am pleased to find it is still half full. That's the difference in my attitude to everything I try to do in my life.

BY WHOSE STANDARDS?

I walked into Mary's house and tripped over an infant-sized yellow wellington lying in the hall. As I put down my weekend bag and took off my coat I mentally adjusted myself to the 'rules of the house', which were not so much rules of behaviour as guidelines for survival. With a toddler around I had to remember not to leave my handbag invitingly open or it would be rifed through when my back was turned, or my hot coffee on the floor where it might cause a nasty burn. From previous visits to Mary's house I know she lives her daily life permanently trying to stem the tide of toys and biscuit crumbs that engulf the whole house, but never quite succeeding. It bothers her a bit, but she finds she has more important things to do with her life than keep the house immaculately clean.

I compare this to one of my clients, Kathy, for whom a neat and sparkling showhouse of a home was the most important thing in her life. She also had a small child but could not come to terms with the fact that it is not natural for babies to be quiet and clean and tidy. Kathy spent every moment of the day running round repairing the ravages her infant created in her island of perfection. The child was given one toy at a time to play with. When he had finished with it that toy was tidied away in a cupboard and another taken out, but while her back was turned in the toy cupboard sticky fingermarks had appeared on the gleaming glass table top, so Kathy would rush to the kitchen for a cloth and the polish to put that right. Basically she was trying to keep her life under control by creating and maintaining total order in her environment – an impossible task. It was not surprising that her eating problems got worse and worse as she tussled with her losing battle.

Kathy had set herself impossibly high standards, and the effort of trying to live up to them had more or less overtaken her ability to see things rationally. She rarely invited people round, and lived in dread of anybody dropping in. What if they should see a toy lying on the floor? The very thought of being caught out in what she saw as failure to keep the house tidy made her almost ill with worry. She imagined scenes where a visitor called and noticed a speck of dust on the mantlepiece or a cushion out of place on the sofa, and the thought made her go cold with panic. She was terrified of appearing less than perfect, and expressed this terror in her compulsive housework. The fact that things were very wrong deep down in Kathy's make-up showed in her compulsive bingeing. This was the only area where she let the tight restrictions weaken from time to time, a pressure valve that blew when she got too steamed up inside.

Personally I would hate to stay the weekend in a house like Kathy's (not that people like that can usually cope with having visitors to stay), her standards of tidiness would be completely beyond me. I drift around all day with a cigarette in one hand and a book in the other, always trying to remember where I put my last cup of coffee down or what I did with the fascinating magazine article I was reading last night. My own flat may look chaotic at times but in fact I usually know where to lay my hands on the information I need, so I have my own kind of order. To have someone rushing round behind me all day long tidying up would probably be disastrous.

We have our own standards for everything, including how tidy or untidy we choose our homes to be. Another friend I stay with regularly has strict ideas about her lifestyle. She does not approve of me smoking in the house, and likes to dress for dinner and serve the right wine with each dish, so I do try to respect her values when I am her guest. Without stifling my own individuality I try to adapt to her expectations of how visitors should behave, or if I don't feel up to coping with that I decline the invitation and stay at home.

Respecting other people's standards has a lot to do with good manners, and one thing that was drummed into me from early childhood was the importance of manners. I suppose I must have rebelled a bit when I was tiny, but what rubbed off was a certain standard of behaviour that is natural to me. Our society puts a lot of store by outwardly acceptable behaviour; too many people don't care about what is going on deep inside as long as what shows on the outside is of the right standard. It is this conflict which is at the root of so many problems. I see it time and again in my clients – those who have developed secret bingeing habits because they find it so hard to equate the turmoil inside with the coping figure they show to the world.

I now see that many alcoholics have the same problem, and so do those who get hooked on drugs. It no longer surprises me when I discover a successful barrister has a chronic drink problem, or a member of one of the country's top families is a drug addict. Nor am I taken in by a well-groomed career woman who comes to consult me; if she needs the Maisner Centre she is a mess inside no matter how tidy the outer shell might appear. All these people are probably brought up from the cradle to live to certain standards of appearances, but if they are basically not temperamentally suited to be that way severe problems begin to develop. Yet how many of us have the confidence and belief in ourselves to set our own standards at a level that suits us as individuals and stick to them no matter what?

It is a fact that people with eating problems often set high standards for themselves and have unrealistic expectations of others. It is not unusual for me to sit through an anguished session with someone who is desperately worried about their eating habits, and then when we get down to analysing their eating charts I find the problem is little more than that they eat one potato too many with their dinner. Then I have to point out to the client that it is not one potato here or there that matters, the real problem is that they are giving themselves so much anxiety and stress over the whole situation. People talk to me about wanting to achieve perfect eating habits. What do they mean by that? Or they say they want to have the perfect figure. Again, what is this ideal of perfection?

'By whose standards' has come to be one of my most often repeated phrases. This endless pursuit of some unrealistic ideal is in most cases just a form of escapism, a bolt-hole from realities that are more difficult to come to terms with. Most compulsive eaters are putting so much energy into thinking about their eating they are able to blot out problems they can't handle, the problems which are really messing up their lives. It is no good for these people to sort out their hang-ups about eating and leave it there; once they begin to get their eating under control there will be space for those other problems to pop up. That is when the real work begins.

'By whose standards?' I say to the girl who tells me she has to be perfectly dressed. Some people might see that as a smart suit and high heels, another as elegant casuals, all these things are relevant. 'By whose standards?' I ask the girl who says she cannot go out to dinner because she does not have perfect table manners. I might tell her the story of the time I was working as a translator on a film set with Orson Welles in Spain, it is a splendid example of people getting the wrong idea about standards of table manners. The Spaniards decided to give a dinner for the British visitors, but someone insisted that the British eat everything with a knife and fork and that was to be the standard of table manners for the evening. I still smile when I picture the poor Spaniards painstakingly dissecting their prawns with a knife and fork while the British guests, unaware of the knife and fork rule, were happily pulling their prawns apart with their fingers.

I lived for a time with a Spanish gypsy, and we often went for an evening meal with his family who lived crowded in little more than a shanty with a dirt floor. One day we arrived straight from the stables, a bit late for dinner, so we hurried straight to the table. 'Paulette hasn't washed her hands', said one horrified member of the family, and I quickly visited the bucket of water by the door provided for that purpose. The family may have lived in circumstances which the likes of me could call squalid, but they had their own standards of hygiene.

It causes so many problems when strong-minded people want to impose their standards on others. And I can't help bringing up the subject of television here. All those slender actresses and model families advertising consumer products are putting over some unrealistic idea of a perfect world, and we are all vulnerable to the pull of it. There are pressure groups popping up that complain about the influence of advertisements or smoking and alcohol, but precious little is said about the evils of some advertisements for food. To promote the sale of biscuits, cakes, pies and sweets the ad men create images of loving families, slender girls, happy social groups, which burrow away at the peace of mind of those of us who lack such trappings of perfection. If loneliness is one root cause of an eating disorder, plugging away an image of eating associated with sitting round the table with a happy family group or a handsome adoring man is only going to exacerbate the problem. It is a subtle form of indoctrination but there is so much of it going on around us all the time that it is not surprising it has such a powerful effect on so many people.

It is not just the advertisers who are to blame; take the average television play or situation comedy show. The characters relate and interact with each other usually in comfortable surroundings and everything generally turns out well in the end. Life is rarely like that but the worlds of fact and fantasy are so close that it is hardly surprising people often find it difficult to distinguish where one ends and the other begins. So many of my clients sincerely believe that if they can just get their eating under control they will 'live happily ever after', like the closing scene of a cowboy film where the baddie has been shot and suddenly everyone is happy and smiling and life is wonderful. I have learnt from long and hard experience that this is just the end of the first scene, the real story is about to start as a life-long work of coming to terms with problems and adjusting and re-adjusting values begins.

We are all taken in by images, not just those manufactured for the screen but the ones that other people throw up around themselves. It is so easy to set your standards of achievement against those you perceive to have been achieved by someone you respect and admire, but that is a very hazardous thing to do. Idols too often turn out to have feet of clay.

For most of my life I went along from day to day accepting the nebulous images of others as solid truth. I judged them and their lives by what I perceived on the surface, and similarly I judged my own life according to what I could see around me. I knew my eating habits and, if I thought about it at all (which I rarely did) I assumed the whole world was the same and that was what food and eating was all about. My way of life was totally geared to my eating habits and I didn't realise there was any other way of living. I had no idea that my state of existing was a recognised medical condition with a name – bulimia nervosa, compulsive eating a condition common to thousands of other people.

Nowadays when I am something of a world expert on the subject and totally dedicated to enlightening people to the fact that such problems are widespread, it surprises people to discover that I had chronic eating problems for years without realising anything was abnormal. It is easy to look back with hindsight and wonder how I could have been so ignorant, but at the time my perception was only what my life to date had prepared me for. Man now *knows* the world is round. Astronauts have been up in space and seen it as a fact and everyone takes this fact for granted. But for thousands of years man, if he considered the subject at all, just assumed the world to be flat, and had no reason to think differently.

Anyone who binges, drinks or takes drugs often lacks a clear concept of any better quality of life. It is almost impossible to bully or force someone to break their compulsive habits just because you see they have a problem; that person has to see the problem for themselves, to adjust their own standards rather than be made to adopt yours. A lonely person goes to the pub for company, a person with no self-confidence drinks and it boosts his self-esteem, so why should he change? Why should he take away those props that make life more bearable unless he can see a real solid benefit?

When I finally got to grips with giving up drinking I went through a lot of suffering. I was so used to reaching for a drink to give me self-confidence that the stark reality of life without that prop was hard to face. Time and again I lost sight of what I was aiming for, I knew I wanted something better out of life but when the need to drink was strong I forgot what could possibly be more important than relief from my present suffering. It was much the same with my struggle to get off Ativan. I had been prescribed it to help me cope with overwhelming pressures, but the pills didn't take the problems away, they just numbed my reaction to them, so when I stopped numbing myself the problems came back. For several weeks whenever the pressure built up my first reaction was to reach for the tranquillisers, even though my logical brain was well aware that I didn't want to be hooked and that I could achieve a better quality of life without them.

The drug support group helped me because I already knew I wanted to stay off. I had already set myself a standard of life without Ativan and just needed help to reinforce it. In the same way clients come to the Maisner Centre because they know they have an eating problem and have decided to do something about it, they need me to show them how to achieve what they want. Nobody would sign up for my course if they did not know they had a problem, they would be totally unaware that their way of life could be different. The way we perceive things at any one time seems to be right to us at that time. It is all very well years later to wish we could wind the clock back and react to situations in our past according to our perception of life today, but that is unrealistic. Maybe ten years from now I will look back at the decisions I am making today and wish I had done things differently, but today I do as I see best for myself, as I am at this moment.

We all see things out of perspective at times, and distort our childhood memories to suit the emotions of the time. A friend of mine was talking recently about his school days. He had been sent away to boarding school at a young age and hated it; he hated the high stone walls that surrounded the bleak school and made it seem like a prison, he hated the long dark corridors and bare echoing classrooms that have always been associated since then in his mind with loneliness and misery. Recently he took a nostalgic drive past his old school to view it through the eyes of age and maturity. What he saw beyond the low mossy walls were acres of green playing fields, it all looked very pleasant and inviting, and so very different from his emotionally charged schoolboy memories.

Making real changes means starting again with new standards and not regretting the past or wanting to try and change what has been. I can't change my father; I never will, any more than I can realistically change my relationship with him, all I can do is change my attitude towards him and try to see the amusing side. I just get on with the things I can achieve instead. I spend a lot of time on the things that matter to me and try to live up to the standards I believe are important for myself. That means I couldn't care less whether I have red or white wine with fish or if my shoes are properly polished, although I know that such things are important to other people, and I do respect those standards. I try to fall in with others as far as good manners dictate, but that is very different from allowing others to inflict their ideas on to me. When I worked as a cook just after I left my husband I felt I had to do things exactly as the lady of the house wanted because I was a live-in servant. She had some ridiculous ideas, for example she made an awful fuss because I used to wring out the tea towels in the wrong direction. She would stand in the kitchen demonstrating how to twist and squeeze the towels and supervising me until I had mastered doing it to her satisfaction. I took it because it never occurred to me to tell her she was a stupid fussy old woman, but how I resented it – and how I crept off to her larder to binge when she wasn't looking.

I allowed her to get to me because I felt vulnerable. It is a lot easier to stick to your guns when you feel confident and on top, but when you are low it is easy to fall victim to other people.

My client Louise was a typical example, she just had no confidence in herself at all and she seemed to give out great waves of vulnerability that begged people to take advantage of her. She would get terribly upset because people at work were always making jokes at her expense or playing unkind tricks on her. It had been exactly the same story at school, the other children used to laugh at her and bully her and steal her sweets. We talked a lot about why she thought people picked on her in particular, and she was adamant that it was just because she was fat; if she could just stop bingeing and lose weight everyone would respect her – after all, nobody teased any of the slim girls in her office. It took a long time to convince her that if she put over the right attitude to others they would not be able to get to her: people only tease those who rise to it and react. We discussed the personalities of the other girls in the office. They were the sort who had enough belief in themselves to shrug off digs and jokes, there was no satisfaction in teasing them because they just did not react. It really had little to do with the size of their bodies but a lot to do with the size of their self-esteem.

People who allow themselves to be teased or bullied or abused because they set their standards so low they don't believe they are worth better, will inevitably get what they ask for. The men who drifted through my life involving me in their problems and hang-ups were the sort I deserved because I did not believe I was worth anything better. Now I think more highly of myself I have become more particular about my friends. I go out socially almost every evening, but I am much more particular about who I go out with. I would rather spend an evening in my own company than with someone so negative they drag me down. My attitude is very different from the days when I was grovelling around buying 'friends' at any price and mixing myself up in other people's problems because that was all I thought I deserved. To be loved and respected by a few worthwhile people is much more satisfying than being tolerated by a large number of second-raters.

I could only reassert my own standards when I rediscovered faith in myself. That is the vital ingredient in succeeding at being your own person, in fact it is vital for any kind of success. So many rich and successful businessmen started out with nothing, no money and often not much education, just a belief in themselves and their ability to come through. Such people set their own values and standards, which may not be the same as other people's, but which they feel to be right for them.

When I set up the Maisner Centre I had total belief in what I was trying to do and in the need for such a enterprise. Otherwise I don't think I would ever have got it off the ground because I found so little support in business circles for something which was new and not obviously commercial. I can picture my bank manager sitting behind his large oak desk looking forward to his pension, with no real concept of what I was talking about. He patted his neat stomach and rattled on about how he sometimes ate too much but then he cut back if he was putting on weight, and other people should do the same. I needed his money, but he was someone who represented everything I was trying to oppose, the attitudes I was determined to break down, the idea that compulsive eaters are just those fat, greedy people who can't resist a second cream bun. He had no understanding of the human misery that rages outside the safe walls of the bank and completely failed to grasp the sincerity and determination of my desire to succeed. Basically he could only see my project in terms of financial returns and it didn't look exactly promising. The solicitor I dealt with was not much better. I later discovered that when he first heard about my work he visualised that I wore a grass skirt and rattled bones. I needed plenty of faith in myself and my work because although I see it as something normal and sensible, so many others just wrote me off as some kind of eccentric.

Fortunately I have managed to prove that the Maisner Centre is something real and important through my success with so many clients and, more recently, recognition from people of influence. Some years ago I reached the finals of the Women Mean Business Awards, a vindication of those who tried to put me down in my early days and a credit to the judges who did not judge the success of the Maisner Centre purely on the yearly balance sheets. I think they were impressed by the fact that I had taken a new idea and turned it into a practical reality, marketed it and brought in a steady flow of clients. Looking at the Maisner Centre as a business, I know that I found a gap in the market, then created a quality product to fill that gap. The fact that I deal in human suffering rather than consumer goods in this respect is irrelevant because I have developed a good service and I run my business to a high standard.

I think it is because of the high standards I set myself in my work that I was invited to go and work for one day a week in one of the London Hospitals. The Maisner Centre was well established in Brighton, I had clients all over the world, many of whom had to do the course purely by post and telephone. It had already been going through my mind that I could reach more people on a personal basis if I was able to operate in London, when the ideal solution came along. An acquaintance of mine had suffered a nervous breakdown and been admitted to hospital in

London. When she recovered she raved about how wonderful the hospital was and what excellent work they did. I sat down and wrote to the hospital telling them about the Maisner Centre and explaining that I thought I could do a good job helping people with eating disorders. They wrote back inviting me to lunch.

I had no trouble producing references from the medical profession about the success of the Maisner Method in helping compulsive eaters. I was less confident about my own qualifications which on paper were far from impressive, but I told them my life story and put over to them the faith I had in my method of work, and that impressed them. To my joy I started working there on a sessional basis. At the same time I arranged to take a room for half a day at a big London health centre, so I would have one full and busy day in London each week. It was an important step forward for me. No business or career can ever stand still, just as no life can stay in one spot for ever, there are always new bridges to cross and new territories to explore.

Perhaps now, after all the battles and heart-searching I have been through, I have the confidence to be myself and do things my way, but years ago doing things my way would have been more an act of rebellion than an expression of self-regard like the time when I was at school in Switzerland and I painted my nails green. Today that is nothing unusual; I believe it is possible to buy green nail varnish at any make-up counter, but then such a thing was unbelievably outrageous. I suppose I did it partly to gain attention and partly to have a dig at my headmistress. She was a rather potty lady; the story was that she had never been the same since she found her husband hanging in the garage. She had a passion for the colour green and painted everything in sight that colour, so to get at her I did my own bit of colouring. Of course it just got me into trouble, but I think it was more than just a silly prank, it was an early expression of me, Paulette the individual. I still love painting my nails, giving myself a manicure is one of my favourite ways of relaxing. I have always had long strong nails, they are a special feature of my appearance so I make the most of them. Bright red nail varnish suits them and sometimes I paint just one nail gold to say to the world in a subtle way 'This is the way I like doing things'.

It is only as I have learnt to respect myself and believe in myself that I have become aware that I can set my own standards in life. I think for most of my past I had no standards at all, in fact I don't think I even knew what the word meant. As a confirmed people-pleaser I just took the course of action which I thought others expected of me without thinking about the consequences to my own life. I cared passionaly what other people thought about me and yet behind closed doors I didn't worry about abusing my body with alcohol, drugs and laxatives. When you are bingeing you don't care about anything except that someone might catch you at it and find out your guilty secret. I suppose the total sum of my philosophy of life over many years was if you were thin you were OK, if you were fat you weren't. Beyond that there was no reality. It is strange that someone whose mind ran constantly on such a restricted track should make friends with a great thinker, but one of my dearest friends during my years in Spain was Bina, who had a deep interest in man and the world.

I was still very much wrapped up in thoughts of being slim and my mind never extended itself further than whether I had enough laxatives, speed and booze to get through the week. Bina was a Buddhist and lived a totally self-sufficient life growing her own food and fetching her own water from the spring. Her home was miles from civilisation and very simple and peaceful. My visits there may well have begun to stir me into looking at what I was making of my own life. We talked and talked and talked, even though we hardly agreed on anything. The joy of talking with Bina was that we could have real two-way conversations, such a change from the usual standard of bar room chat I was used to where people just talk at each other and nobody really listens to what is being said. We discussed all sorts of things from Buddhism, to food and nourishment, to men, and I found her company stimulating and inspiring. She never converted me to her religious beliefs, although I still think that if I were to adopt any formal religion it would be Buddhism. Bina was not the type to try and convert anyone, any more than she would have tried to bully me to come off alcohol even though she did not drink herself. She had travelled a lot, including spending some time in the Himalayas, and she had developed her own philosophy of life and her own standards by which she lived regardless of what might be going on in the rest of the world. Her influence on me, I think, was not that she imposed her standards on me but that she sparked the idea that I must develop my own style and remain true to it. That takes a lot of self-confidence, a quality I was severely short of in those days.

If Bina could see me smart and confident walking into my office in a big London hospital to start work, she would be happy for me. She would approve of me discovering what I truly believe in and pushing ahead to achieve it, even though she herself still prefers to live in the peaceful seclusion of rural Spain. I try hard to get this across to my clients; to show them that they do not need to live according to other people's values and expectations, the most important thing is that they are true to themselves. So many unrealistic expectations are brought to my door by young girls and middle-aged women who think that is what the world expects of them. All I can do is try to impress on them that standards have to be realistic and must take into account that everyone is human, with ups and downs and strengths and weaknesses.

Often as I am talking to people I tell them about things that I have done, events that have happened to me in the past which are relevant to their situation. They think I am talking about myself but in fact it is as if I am telling them about another person, one of the other two women who share in this personality that is Paulette, neither of which are really me. I have always worked like this, but I only recently became fully aware that I see myself in this triple way. My new awareness has helped to open my eyes to a lot of things about myself, which was something I certainly would not have been able to handle a few years ago. I am discovering other sorts of problems are coming forward for me to face and deal with. In a way it is like taking the next stage on from the kind of course clients follow with the Maisner Method. I long ago realised that I used to binge and drink and swallow pills instead of sorting out my problems, and I think I have come to terms with all of that. Now I am ready to dig a bit deeper.

It all began when I decided I wanted to give up smoking. I think I had already reached a point in my life when I was ready to find an even greater self-awareness, but the smoking issue gave me a point to focus on. It was the first time in my life I had seriously considered weaning myself off cigarettes. Until then I had considered them an integral part of my life, as I have always smoked. Although I know all the facts and figures about smoking and health, because I don't have a cough and I can swim a good distance without getting breathless I don't find that side of the issue a real motivation to give up. With me it is more a need to feel I am not ruled by cigarettes, that I don't need them to get through the day.

I soon discovered that a major reason why I was smoking so many cigarettes was that I sleep so badly, and I need cigarettes to help me through the restless, lonely hours of the night. I thought I should work on my sleeplessness before tackling the smoking problem, and it was while looking at my sleeplessness and what lies behind it that a clear picture began to emerge of how I see the polarities of my personality, two extreme people quite separate from me and from each other.

At this point I decided to see a therapist. Through him I was guided away from the idea that my career was the only thing in my life; he showed me that I had needs as a person and that this was OK, which was something I knew but on my own had not fully reached the point of accepting. I began taking L-Tryptophan, a non-addictive substance that I had known about for years but never tried, always assuming it was something that would work for others but not for me. My sleeping patterns improved dramatically, much to my surprise.

I have also come to terms with the fact that I don't really want to give up smoking at this point in my life. I had said I did because other people were putting pressure on me. I gave up my other addictions when the time arrived when I knew I wanted to. If and when the day comes when I want to give up smoking, then and only then will I succeed in doing it.

As my therapy progressed I watched how the three people that are Paulette began to grow closer together and merge more into one. It took a lot of time and hard work, but it did happen.

I have observed time and time again in people who come to the Maisner Centre for help that their whole personality seems to be split in half, the successful social exterior struggling with the tortured inner soul on the battleground of eating habits. Such people hardly know who the real self is – a feeling I know so very well. So many girls arrive to see me for that first consultation drawing on all their reserves of social training to get them through the ordeal. They are usually at a point of desperation, but to meet me they have put on their best clothes, ensured hair, nails and make-up are immaculate, and screwed themselves up to a high pitch of brightness and breeziness.

If I had not spent years doing exactly the same sort of thing myself and watching others do it, I could well have been taken in by Anne the first time she bounced into my office. She was so eager to tell me all about her marvellous job in the City as private secretary to an up and coming executive. She told me how he worked hard and long and expected his staff to match him in zeal and dedication, so Anne made sure she was always there to take his notes, answer his telephone and tidy his desk at the end of the day. In fact she devoted herself entirely to making herself indispensable to him.

Eventually we got round to the reason for her visiting the Maisner Centre. Apparently the one cloud in Anne's blue sky was her eating problem. At the weekends when there was no work, no boss, no office to go to, she would find herself bingeing. If only she did not binge at weekends everything would be marvellous she said.

On this first interview I was being shown the successful working girl side of Anne, but the next time she came it was a very different personality who walked through the door. Crumpled and unwashed, she was letting me see the other Anne, the one who was ruthlessly barred form the executive suite. This was the lonely unhappy girl with nothing in her life but her job, nobody to care about her or need her, just a boss who hardly noticed she was anything more than an office machine.

The bright successful Anne existed from nine to five Monday to Friday, but the rest of the time she was an unhappy bingeing Anne who lacked friends, hobbies, ambitions and any sense of personal fulfillment. In coming to terms with why she binged at weekends, she had to recognise this unhappy Anne and give her the stimulation to become an emotionally fulfilled person in her own right. As long as she had no other interests in life apart from her work, a part of her remained empty and hungry. Somewhere between the two extremes of Anne which I saw in front of me was the true Anne who had to learn to be in control of her own life and in control of her eating.

Anne was too extreme in living only for her working hours. But I have learnt that being successful in a career must almost inevitably mean making certain sacrifices in one's personal life. The same rules apply here as in every difficult personal situation in life which has to be faced: first see the situation clearly, then make the choice as to what you truly want and whether you can accept the consequences of that choice. For some people the price of reaching the top is just too high, the ultimate success is ruined by the severe personal toll it takes to achieve it. I am thinking in particular of the sad case of Raquel who had a rare gift for dancing and worked long and hard to achieve fame as a top ballet dancer. While her body moved in total rhythm her emotions became jangled and discordant, she became hooked on eating and the only way she could maintain the slender build essential to her art was by making herself sick. She became severely bulimic, very ill and desperately unhappy. The price she paid for her success was more than she could afford. On the surface it looked quite simple, her career demanded she be extremely slim so she made herself sick if she ate too much. But it was soon revealed as something much deeper, a tortuous muddle of ambition, frustration, lack of confidence and sheer panic. The pressures of getting to the top and staying there drained her emotionally, leaving her empty inside so she was compelled to binge to fill that emptiness. The weight problem was an excuse to cop out of the personal pressures surrounding her lifestyle that were more than she could handle.

Concentrating on my career and devoting the past years to learning as much as possible about my subject has meant making a number of sacrifices but none that I really regret. My social life has changed but it is not a change for the worse. Because I am altogether more in control of my life I can choose my friends and my entertainment with, I hope, more wisdom. I make sure I have time to spend with my friends, and when I feel I have had enough of work I stop, because I have made the choice that I am no longer going to work as hard as I did in the early days of setting up the Centre. I go to the theatre regularly, and make time to go out to lunch with friends when I am invited, because I now respect myself enough to allow myself to enjoy these occasions instead of indulging in the guilty feeling that I should always be at the beck and call of work.

Because I respect myself more, I find myself more and more surrounded by the sort of friends whom I can respect, while many of those I used to call my friends in the old days seem to have slipped away. There were no big rows and bust-ups, just a gradual awareness that we seemed to have little in common any longer. The people I used to call my friends were those who took drugs or were alcoholics, in other words they were failures, and I was a failure. Now I am discovering I can be successful at living my life and my friends are people who are also successful in their own ways.

About twelve years ago I was talking to a therapist friend and bemoaning the fact that every man I knew either took drugs or was an alcoholic, was unemployed or a workaholic, in fact they all had some kind of personality problem. 'Are there no normal men in the world?', I asked. He told me the truth, although at the time I scoffed at what he said; he told me that I was sick and so I attracted sick people, and when I was well I would attract people who were healthy. How true that has proved to be: the friends who were so sick have fallen away and the ones I have kept are those with a strong and healthy grasp on life.

Although I have changed a lot over the years I am still Paulette, and I am still just as human, even though some people see me as someone very different and tend to shy away. The smart successful Paulette chooses to let it be like that, while the other Paulette is often surprised by the way people allow themselves to be dazzled by the successful image. If people see me as perfect and unattainable, someone I am not, it is not because I actively project a false image but because they choose to see me in a certain way. Certain people don't want to know anything but a perfect Paulette set up on a pedestal above the rest of the world and out of intimate reach; their own insecurities build up this image.

The particular example of this which comes to mind is a girl called Carole who came for consultations about eating problems compounded by a range of emotional problems and lack of self-confidence. On the third consultation she suddenly burst out with how much she hated me, which rather knocked me back, but I pursued the line of talk and asked her why she hated me. Her hatred was based on the fact that she had an image of me as being beautifully groomed, which was difficult for me to come to terms with, especially as at that time I was going though a phase of wearing jeans and tartan shirts, hardly the height of Paris couture. I pursued the question still further, trying to find out why she saw me as being well-groomed, and after a long pause for thought she said it was because my nails were perfect ... Carole's need to put me out of reach on a pedestal, so that she could cope with the help and advice I was giving her, was such that she blanked out the casual dress and the disorganised office, and concentrated only on the one thing she could see that confirmed the image she needed to conjure up.

This story helps to add weight to one of the techniques we use in the Maisner Method. I tell people that everyone has some feature they can be proud of, but usually they are so totally engrossed in the flabbiness of their thighs or the size of their waist they are totally unaware of the rest of their body. Nice hands have always been a special feature of mine so I make sure my nails are always well-manicured to make the best of a good feature. Look at the result – a client sees only my well-groomed nails and does not really notice the rest of me. I see so many people who are completely obsessed with fat arms, a big nose or a large bust they think everyone else must be as conscious of the feature as they are themselves. In fact others often do not even notice. What the person with the obsession is doing is using one feature as a peg to hang all their deep-seated insecurities and lack of self-esteem on.

Many years ago, I can't have been more than 20 years old, I was walking on the beach with a boyfriend of the time called Dennis. Looking down at our toes half buried in the sand Dennis idly observed, 'Don't shoes hide a multitude of sins'. In my insecurity I gazed at my feet and saw them as ugly and misshapen. I developed quite a complex about my feet and dreaded people seeing them. It was only recently when I was in hospital with back problems that a nurse said to me, 'Haven't you got nice feet?'. Suddenly it all fell into place: Dennis all those years ago had been talking about *his* feet, not *mine*. I had let more than half a lifetime go by carrying a complex based on a misunderstanding.

There are no end of stories about people who have plastic surgery believing that when they have a cute little nose everyone will begin to love them, but when the bruises subside and the bandages come off they are just the same person underneath. Then they begin to think they must do something about the shape of their ears so that they will be universally admired. The girl who believes her husband will give her more attention if she is slim starts to diet, then discovers the relationship is no better so she slims down even more, until she is so caught up in eating problems and bulimia the marriage is at risk of breaking down completely. Almost nothing is solved by altering the outside features, it is inside that the changes have to take place.

Although I have been successful at improving the quality of my life, that does not mean I don't still have problems and down days. In fact success brings a whole new crop of problems such as responsibility to others and financial burdens.

On my first serious attempt to cut down my smoking I found it very hard, especially at times of stress when the habit of a lifetime was to reach out for a cigarette. People kept remarking how irritable and bad tempered I was, and when I told them it was because I was trying to give up smoking they accepted this explanation with relief, making remarks like 'Thank God you're not perfect, I can talk to you'. That old Paulette with all her faults and failings is the one who related to people with serious problems. I know I do lose my temper and get irritable, but the real deep problems that cast such a dark shadow over my life are gone, left behind in the past, and I no longer binge, so I can say to people who want to be like me that nobody can ever be perfect but at least they can discover what it is like to be human.

With many people it is the sheer frustration of a way of life that does not truly suit them which is at the root of their problems, and so they project on to me all their dreams of self-fulfilment. They see me as in control, happy, successful, because that is what they are seeking for themselves. For them I must be the perfect end result of the course they are about to undertake, they don't want to know that I still have problems: if I have not reached perfection by practising what I preach, what hope is there for them? By their very nature compulsive eaters are usually all-or-nothing people who can only visualise the depths of misery or total bliss and have no real concept of an ordinary, human, up-and-down existence.

When people say they want to be like me, it is not the real me they are seeking to copy – how can it be, because they don't know my inner secret self, they only meet the outer image. It is the image they project on to me that they want to be like, and it can be hard work acting as a projection screen for so many different home movies.

Ken, who is a teacher, is perhaps typical of this. Like many of my clients from the teaching profession he appears to be doing well in his career, but underneath he is frustrated and unhappy.

He feels the limitations of his work, the lack of opportunity to use his intellect to the full. As he sees his life slipping away along with all the hopes and dreams of his youth, he is becoming embittered. In talking with Ken about his eating problems we discuss skills he has forgotten he possessed, and try to explore all the potential which is lying untouched and fuelling his frustration.

Ken does not want to see me on one of my bad days, he has enough bad days of his own to cope with. He would not allow me to look as tired and battered as he does, to leave a week's washing up in the sink as he does, to watch television all evening instead of preparing the next day's work as he does. If I do all these things Ken does not want to know. With the compulsive eater's intense ability to see only his own problems, he needs to believe I have risen above such things so I can guide him out of the mess he has made of his life.

And yet others in turn might envy Ken his success and his university degree. His long and distinguished career which, by years of plodding on has brought him to the post of headmaster of a good school, is an achievement which many would covet. He is respected and trusted in the community and children and parents project on to him the image of the headmaster they want for their school.

So what is success? The dictionary tells me it is the accomplishment of an end aimed at. By that definition Ken, who set out to become a headmaster, is a success even though he feels some essential part of life has escaped him. I too, who opened the Maisner Centre to help people with their eating problems and have become an expert on the subject, could also define myself as successful. Yet to describe my life in that way implies that I have come to the end of a journey, reached some kind of final goal, whereas I am still very much on the road and off to explore new territories. Perhaps I have not achieved success yet, or have achieved it without fully realising that I have done so. Certainly if this is the ultimate point of success in my life I shall feel cheated because I am optimistic of achieving more in the years ahead.

How does one assess degrees of success? I see people like Ken who appear to the world as successful and yet feel themselves to be failures, and I come across others who appear content with a life which others would call failure. One of my favourite characters in Brighton is someone I call the Gentle Giant. I think he is an alcoholic, possibly a drug addict, and I often catch sight of him sitting on a bench or crashed out on the beach. Shoppers and tourists give him a wide berth as he weaves along, but he always gives me a nod and a smile when I pass and there is something peaceful and contented about his face which makes me think he is at peace with himself and the world.

It is a mistake to judge my own success by other people's assessment of me; others put too much of their own ideals and prejudices into their judgement to make their opinions accurate. I need to establish my own standards and judge my performance by those, because I am the only one who knows myself well enough to make true assessment. On the one hand I am faced with some clients who see me as the ultimate success because I have my eating under control, while at the same time my own father despairs of me because I have not become wealthy through my work and by his standards I am therefore a total failure. In my own eyes I am at neither extreme, but somewhere in the middle.

The danger of judging success by one's own standards is that those standards are likely to be set impossibly high, especially when you are the sort of person who tends towards compulsive eating or some kind of extreme behaviour. Kate, for example, started the course and did very well for two weeks, then a crisis arose in her life and she turned to food for support. Instead of learning from it and putting it all behind her the next day and carrying on with her course, she told herself she was a complete and total failure because she had binged once and so she gave up completely, thus allowing herself to plunge back into all her old bad habits.

Kate had a need to see herself as a failure and was only looking for an excuse to binge so that she could prove to herself her inability to succeed. I worked with her on why she needed to fail time and time again, and we covered the attitude of her parents who expected too much of their only child, and later talked through the stress of a demanding husband and children who she allowed to walk over her. Kate's bingeing is still as bad as ever because she is not prepared to sort out these problems, she is too afraid of what it might mean to see herself as successful.

Fear of success is as common as fear of failure. While it is easier to understand and even admit to a fear of failing at any particular task or at life in general, it is more difficult to understand why people are so terrified of becoming successful. I find myself panicking sometimes when I look at my career and the success I have achieved. For me there is a distinct fear that I may have reached the end of the road, that I may have achieved as much as I can in my career and there is nothing left ahead of me. Now that Harley Street psychiatrists refer people to me for help, and I am even quoted in medical magazines, where do I go from here? After spending so much of my life dragging myself painfully up the stairway of success, the penthouse is quite an exposed and frightening place to be.

I am definitely not alone in my fear of success. Time and again I see other people setting themselves impossible challenges at which there is no risk of them achieving success. Sometimes they are aware of what they are doing, but usually it is done instinctively without any real awareness of how their mind is operating. It is all part of this tendency to live to extremes which is common to so many of the Maisner Centre's clients: success must be complete and surpassing all others, failure is total and despairing. Eating is either bingeing or starving, the in-between of controlled eating habits is alien to their nature because it is too ordinary and unchallenging to hold any appeal.

Sally is a typical example of this, and I have spent many hours on the telephone listening to her problems. She tells me she has to be the best, she has to achieve perfection in everything she does, which of course is quite unrealistic, so she ends up doing nothing. She can't allow visitors to drop in in case the house is less than perfectly clean and tidy, she can't allow herself to invite friends round for dinner in case the meal she prepares in some way falls short of her ideals of perfection. Instead of doing ordinary things in an average way she cops out completely from doing anything and spends much of her life in bed eating. I talk to her about the benefits of failure, how people will like her more if they see she has a few human failings, how we learn about ourselves and life from our mistakes. But Sally firmly believes that she can only be accepted by others if she is perfect and ultimately successful in every way.

Although I know I am successful in my career, there are other areas of my life in which I feel I have not been as successful as I would wish, and this is something I still need to come to terms with and perhaps set up as a goal to achieve in the future.

One day it occurred to me that I had spent so much time working, so many days listening to other people's problems, that it was time to do something for me. I had reached a point where life seemed empty, people bored me, and I was becoming less sympathetic towards my clients and their problems. I have always believed that if you find people in general boring, it is often not them who are at fault but yourself, so I accepted that I needed to liven up my life to rediscover how interesting people can be.

'Where do I meet like-minded people?', I found myself asking. To start with I looked up details of a seminar on Life Enhancement which I had heard about some years earlier and vaguely planned to do some day. Now I felt that day had come. I booked my place and went along. It was exhausting, draining, overwhelming, but it was exciting, challenging and inspiring. I came away physically shattered, but on fire with a new enthusiasm for living. Even more important, I met half a dozen interesting and stimulating people who I am sure will be an influence in my life in future years. None of this would have come about if I had sat at home listening to my excuses for restricting my life.

I know how traumatic it can be when people are forced to face up to the realisation that they have not made the kind of success of their lives that they set out to achieve. Such a person is Joan who worked for the same company all her life and never gained the promotion she had set her heart on. By the time she reached retirement age she was set into a pattern of bingeing, and she then added her failure to lose weight to her list of failures in life. She needed to come to terms with what she had achieved, which was a very decent contribution to the company in the working posts she had held, and also accept that she had not reached certain goals but in the long run that did not matter. I talked to her about the future, about all the things pensioners can do when they are free from the daily grind of going to the office, and tried to change her obsession with the past into plans for the future.

Even the mundane practicalities of success have their own problems. Although I am inspired by a day's work in London and on fire with enthusiasm the sheer physical effort of it is sometimes difficult to handle. I must get up at six to catch the London train, and a 17-hour day lies ahead before I stagger back drained and exhausted to my flat in Brighton. Sometimes I think I won't be able to handle it, I panic that I will arrive without the right papers because, not being a particularly organised person, I can get into a muddle over apparently simple things like packing my briefcase. I know I am like this, I recognise that this is a characteristic of my personality, so I try and devise a way round it. It is not unknown for me to pack my briefcase on Friday to be sure of having it correct on Monday morning and it is amazing how this can save me a lot of worry and stress through the weekend. A trick as simple as this can take so much pressure off a stressful situation, and I think quite a lot of successful people are those who have mastered such things, they recognise their weak points and devise ways round them instead of doggedly forcing themselves to handle difficult situations in the obvious way. Not that I could ever see myself as some kind of Superwoman: I am much too disorganised by nature, and I don't believe in tying myself up in knots trying to be some super-efficient executive which I clearly am not.

At times it did not seem possible to me that I could be truly successful in my work because of my lack of educational qualifications, I don't have as much as an O level to flaunt, yet I can honestly say this has never really stood in my way. When I was first faced with the prospect of working in a London hospital alongside people with strings of letters after their names I felt daunted by their outward displays of academic success. But I brought myself round to the idea that it was essential for me to think positively about the situation, and this was firmly reinforced on my first day when a top doctor commented: 'You are better qualified in this field than any of us, you have been there.'

It is well-known that the top can be a lonely place, as many successful people have discovered. Just look at the unhappy secret lives of people like Elvis Presley, or the loneliness of Judy Garland – both of whom suffered from eating disorders. Perhaps this is another reason for fearing success. I can say now that I am not lonely because I do have some good friends and I have a sense of fulfilment. Being with people I like and respect from time to time is very different from my old habit of surrounding myself with unsatisfactory people just so I would not be alone. I could feel lonely in a whole crowd of my former 'friends' who were not worthwhile companions. I think it is because I have succeeded in liking myself that I can be content with my own company. When I total up the list of my successes in life perhaps this is the most important one, and the one which gives me the most satisfaction.

When I am at work in London I really feel I am part of a team, worthy to be one of the group of men and women who work together, and this is vitally important to me. Others speak to me as an equal as we discuss mutual clients and methods of helping them, and I can feel proud of being who I am. For me this is the real meaning of success.

It is not selfish to value yourself and respect your own wants and needs. What I would call selfish is being so wrapped up in your own problems that you become oblivious to the rest of the world. Once I began to realise that I am a worthwhile part of the world I could begin to relate to others and value and respect my fellow human beings. When a person can do that, they are really in a position to give help to those who need it, whether it is by launching a campaign to feed the world's starving millions or giving a poor down-and-out two pence to help him buy a meat pie. You can't achieve things for other people until you have achieved a love and respect for yourself.

For all those years my chief waking thought was how to be slim, I never really liked myself and was never satisfied with any of the things I did achieve, and I can recognise the same old thought patterns whizzing around in the brains of one after another of my clients. If being thin had been a serious practical ambition unclouded by a mish-mash of emotional and psychological problems, I would no doubt have achieved it. Just as my uncomplicated bank manager, when I tried to tell him about the need for a centre for eating disorders, patted his trim stomach and agreed he sometimes ate too much and had to cut back if he found he was putting on a bit of weight. He could shed a few extra pounds whenever it suited him because weight was not an emotional issue with him. Compulsive eaters are anything but uncomplicated: they set themselves goals which somewhere deep down they know to be impossible to achieve so that they can then fill up their unhappy empty lives with a vain struggle.

Ambitions have to be sorted out into those which are practical and attainable and those which are merely pipe dreams. As far as the attainable ones are concerned the next step is to analyse what is stopping you getting where you want to go.

Let me use myself as an example. If someone were to ask me today what my main ambition at the moment is, I might well reply that I want a house with a garden. If that is my overwhelming desire at this present time, why am I not at this very moment in the estate agent's office putting my flat up for sale and collecting details of suitable houses to buy? Of course, it is just not as simple as that. When faced with putting my dreams into real action I begin to come up with a list of excuses:

● I am too busy to go house hunting.

● I have a bad back and can't face all that packing.

● My ceilings were damaged in the hurricane and I have not sorted out the insurance claim yet.

● My flat is handy for my work and easy for staff and clients to reach.

● I can't afford the sort of house I would like in Brighton.

● Moving to a less expensive area would mean giving up many things I enjoy, like theatres and a swimming pool on my doorstep.

The list goes on, and while none of these excuses is really insurmountable, for one reason or another I dither about moving and just keep extending my forest of indoor plants. so obviously, moving house is not really an important issue at the moment.

I also wonder, if I did move to this house and garden I dream of, whether it would be what I wanted. It would not be a little Garden of Eden, there would be weeds and slugs, the digging would murder my back and I might have shocking neighbours. Nowadays I can sit back and view the whole question clearly; I no longer get so carried away with enthusiasm for a new plan that I refuse to see all sides of the situation. Moving house would just be an alteration of my lifestyle which would bring me advantages and disadvantages. Wherever I live I will take myself along, so if I like myself I have the chance of being reasonably happy anywhere; if I had no self-esteem I would manage to be miserable in paradise.

Time and time again the same type of person comes walking through my door. She is a girl who does not like herself for whatever reason, lacks confidence to make something of her life, lacks the assertiveness to throw off the people and things which are dragging her down. She is a girl who constantly thinks about eating, is always trying to diet, always breaking down into binges, never happy or content. She is still in the elevator going down and unless she is prepared to make changes she will remain stuck in that stifling cage.

But the opportunity is there – she can choose to make the changes and take the first step out of the cage.

I know it can be done, because I have done it. It took many years for the penny to drop, and many more of struggling up and slipping back, but as I take a look at my life and my attitudes now I can truly say I have made it back to the penthouse.

PART 2

LIFE
IS AN
ELEVATOR

INTRODUCTION

Once the penny has dropped – once you realise you have a problem, and have reached the stage where you can say, 'Enough is enough.' I want to make changes: I am ready to make changes!', then you are ready to help yourself climb back up towards the penthouse.

This part of the book outlines the self-help programme that I advocate at the Maisner Centre.

The first and most important step is to start treating yourself as you would a friend. You may know someone who is completely disorganised, whose house is always a tip, who smokes like a chimney, but, if she is a friend, you like her despite her faults, don't you? If you kept on telling her you thought she was a slob, you'd pretty soon be minus one friend, wouldn't you?

So why treat yourself like that?

Learn to like yourself. Once you can say, 'I am a nice person. I deserve better,' you can begin to look after yourself properly – which is the next important step.

Once you have raised your self-esteem and started looking after yourself properly, you will be fit, both physically and psychologically, to cope with making the changes in lifestyle that you are aiming for.

DO YOU HAVE AN EATING DISORDER?

This questionnaire has been taken from *The Food Trap* by Paulette Maisner and Rosemary Turner.

	Sometimes	Yes	No
1. (a) Do you have panic desires for certain foods?			
(b) Do you recognise real physical hunger?			
(c) If you do, do you eat when you are not hungry?			
(d) Are you fully aware of what you eat?			
2. Do you look forward with pleasure and anticipation to the moment when you can eat alone?			
3. Do you eat sensibly before others and make up for it alone?			
4. Do you have feelings of guilt and remorse every time you eat?			
5. Do you have feelings of guilt and remorse every time you over-eat?			
6. Do you plan your secret binges ahead of time?			
7. If you were eating a cake or sweets, could you eat only half and leave the rest? (eg. could you leave, say, half a Mars bar?)			
8. Do you enjoy cooking for others, although you do not enjoy eating what you have cooked?			
9. Do you avoid socialising because of your inability to cope with food?			

	Sometimes	Yes	No
10. Do you find it difficult to refuse food when pressed?			
11. When eating with others, do you eat the same as everyone else because you are embarrassed to ask for what you know is better for you?			
12. Do you feel awkward when eating with others?			
13. Are your table manners the same when you eat alone as they are when you eat in public?			
14. Are you able to leave food on your plate?			
15. Are your eating habits costing you an excessive amount of money?			
16. Are you ever afraid to weigh yourself?			
17. Do you think about food and your weight constantly?			
18. Does your well-being depend on whether you have a 'good' eating day or 'bad' eating day?			

Add your score as follows:

	Sometimes	Yes	No		Sometimes	Yes	No
1. (a)	1	2	0	9.	2	4	0
(b)	1	0	2	10.	2	4	0
(c)	1	2	0	11.	2	4	0
(d)	1	0	2	12.	2	4	0
2.	2	4	0	13.	2	0	4
3.	2	4	0	14.	2	0	4
4.	2	4	0	15.	2	4	0
5.	2	4	0	16.	1	2	0
6.	2	4	0	17.	2	4	0
7.	2	0	4	18.	1	2	0
8.	2	4	2				

Now answer these questions and add them to your score: Put the relevant number in the appropriate box and add numbers to your total score

1. How many slimming magazines have you read in the last few months?

2. How many diets have you tried in the last 12 months?

3. By how many pounds has your weight fluctuated in the past 12 months in an excess of 5lb, not including premenstrual days?

4. How many times have you joined a slimming club?

5. How many times a week do you weigh yourself?

What your score means:

Score of 0–10 It is obvious you do not have an eating disorder of any description. Lucky you!

Score of 10–50 It is most likely you are suffering to a certain degree with an eating disorder, whether or not you are admitting this fact to yourself.

Over 50 You will have to face up to the fact that you have an eating problem sooner or later, if you have not done so already. Now is the time to do something positive. Contact The Maisner Centre for Eating Disorders, Box 464 Hove, East Sussex, BN3 2BN. Telephone: Brighton (0273) 729818/ 29334.

SELF-ESTEEM

When a baby is born it is aware only of itself, its immediate wants and needs. Then as it grows it learns that it is only one part of a very big world and it loses that first conviction of self-importance. As the child gets older it is likely on average that it will be put down by parents and other grown ups more often than it receives encouragement and praise. The rules of our culture dictate that it is conceited to say things like 'I am pretty' or 'I am clever'. So we do not learn to like ourselves. Instead, we build up a negative image of ourselves which clouds our ability to develop realistic self-knowledge.

It becomes a habit to believe everything that others tell you.

For example:

> A parent tells a child he is clumsy and always breaks everything he touches. The child believes this often repeated message and never tries to find out whether he can be clever with his hands.

With low self-esteem all experiences and communications are interpreted in the most negative form, any criticism is taken badly.

For example:

> A concerned friend remarks, 'You're looking pale, are you feeling OK?' The person with low self-esteem interprets this as 'I look a mess, my friend thinks I'm not bothering to make an effort to look good. That is because I am so lazy and useless. She probably does not want to be friends with me any more.'

The negative is placed before the positive every time, obscuring the person's many good qualities and achievements. For example:

> The woman who has a good job and is complimented on her work replies, 'But I am not a good wife and mother, I don't spend enough time cleaning the house and taking

the children out'.

PERFECTIONISM

Too often the belief develops that it is necessary to be perfect:

People will only respect me and like me if I am perfect.'

This attitude can leave a person lonely. They are afraid to let others see them as anything less than perfect so they avoid many social situations. They can also easily alienate others by appearing to have no human emotions or frailties. The great fear of rejection, 'because I am not perfect', which this person feels holds them back from seeking out relationships.

DO YOU SUFFER FROM LOW SELF-ESTEEM?

In these following examples, answers (a) and (b) show low self-esteem while answers (c) and (d) show good self-esteem.

1. Someone says 'That's a pretty dress'. You reply:

    (a) Do you really think so?

    (b) It was secondhand; it didn't cost much.

    (c) Thank you.

    (d) Yes, it is a nice colour and style, isn't it?

2. Are you afraid to charge enough for your services? When you go for a job interview do you:

    (a) Ask for less than the going rate.

    (b) Accept whatever wage is offered without question.

    (c) Ask the going rate.

(d) Ask for more than the going rate because you know you are worth it.

3. Do you always assume everything is your fault? If your marriage breaks down do you:

(a) Assume it is all your fault.

(b) Assume all your friends will think it is your fault.

(c) Accept there are failings and problems on both sides.

(d) Accept he is a violent man and you are better without him.

4. Fear of rejection is very common in people with low self-esteem. It's your birthday. You wonder about asking your colleagues to celebrate with you at the pub. Do you:

(a) Forget the idea; they would probably turn you down anyway.

(b) Ask one person, but then drop the idea if she turns you down.

(c) Ask several people, not minding if some of them say 'No'.

(d) Make a public announcement and lead the way to the pub.

OTHER SIGNS OF LOW SELF-ESTEEM

● Always attracting people into your life who put you down.

● Being unable to make decisions because you are sure you will be wrong.

● When someone else is irritable, you wonder what you have

done to cause it.

● When you don't hear from someone you assume you have done something to upset them.

● Feeling guilty about spending time or money on yourself.

● Always running around trying to please other people.

● If you don't match up to a top model or famous actress in the way you look you see yourself as inferior.

HOW TO MAKE CHANGES

Banishing a lifetime's habit of low self-esteem will not be achieved overnight. It needs working on. You can make a start with these exercises:

1. If someone who really loved you was talking about you, what qualities would they say you had? Make a list, and write them down. For example:

   I am a good listener

   I have nice eyes

2. Stand in front of a mirror, look yourself in the eyes and say with conviction 'I love you just as you are'. This is something that should be repeated over and over again, even if you feel you don't believe it to begin with.

3. Make a short list of things you want for yourself, e.g. More money; A good relationship; A better job. Then add 'I DESERVE THESE THINGS'

   i.e. I deserve to have more money

   I deserve a good relationship

I deserve a better job

4. Make a list of three flaws which you see as major contributions to your negative self-image, e.g.

   I am untidy

   rewrite this as:

   My untidiness is a part of me ... I am not my untidiness

5. Have some tolerance for yourself. Learn to forgive your own shortcomings in the same way as you would forgive others in the same situation.

6. Join a group or workshop on low self-esteem. It is easier to learn to make the necessary changes in a group environment with professional guidance.

SELF-ASSERTIVENESS

Self-assertiveness is about realising we all have certain rights as human beings. Asserting yourself means being honest with yourself and others and dealing with others on equal terms. It is a way of feeling good about yourself because you have respect for yourself. It does not mean being aggressive; there is no need for aggression when you can assert yourself in an appropriate manner.

In any situation there can be three basic styles of behaviour:

● Aggressive

● Passive

● Assertive

Aggressive behaviour may take the form of violence or threats, or more generally behaving with no regard for, or even awareness of, the feelings of others. By contrast *passive* behaviour causes the person to allow themselves to be pushed around and, as a result, to store up internal loads of resentment and anger.

In *assertive* behaviour the person considers the feelings of others while standing up for themselves and communicating their true feelings clearly. There is no need to feel guilty or under stress for acting in one's own best interests.

For example, how would you respond in the following situations:

1. You are at the hairdresser's. The stylist holds up the mirror to show you the finished style and you think it looks dreadful. Do you:

(a) Get angry and storm out saying you will never come to that salon again. *(Aggressive)*

(b) Say 'Thank you, that's lovely' and rush home in tears to re-do it. (*Passive*)

(c) Say 'I realise you have done your best; however, I don't think the style suits me swept back off my forehead. I would like you to re-style the front into a fringe'. *(Assertive)*

2. After supper the family rushed off to watch television, leaving you to wash up alone. Do you:

(a) Storm in and unplug the set yelling at them they are lazy and selfish. *(Aggressive)*

(b) Do all the washing up yourself, seething with resentment. *(Passive)*

(c) Say 'I want to pop next door to see Janet, will you please do the washing up when this programme is over' *(Assertive)*

3. You order your steak rare in a restaurant and it comes well done. Do you:

(a) Shout at the waiter, 'This steak is terrible! Don't you ever listen to people when they give orders? I am not paying for this'. *(Aggressive)*

(b) Eat it, but the whole meal is ruined for you. *(Passive)*

(c) Say 'I ordered my steak rare, this is well done, please will you get me another one'. *(Assertive)*

Was your response usually the passive one?

In a situation where people keep trying to push you into doing something you don't want to do, the 'broken record' technique is very effective:

'Have a cake'

'No thank you, I don't want one'

'They're very nice, do have one'

'No thank you, I don't want one'

'I made them specially for you'

'No thank you, I don't want one'

'Go on, just have one'

'No thank you, I don't want one'

The trick is never to veer from your original statement even though the conversation begins to become tedious. Once you start to change your statement, for example if you begin to justify what you say be adding 'I'm on a diet', you are no longer being totally self-assertive.

Requests

Making or refusing requests of others can be an area full of difficulties and pitfalls for the victim of low self-esteem. Some people find it almost impossible either to ask for anything or to say 'No'.

Making Requests

1. Remember, you have a right to make your wants known to others.

2. When you do not ask for what you want, you deny your own importance.

3. The best chance you have of getting exactly what you want is by asking for it specifically and directly. If you ask indirectly or drop hints, you run the risk of not being heard or understood and your request may go unheeded as a consequence.

Refusing Requests

1. Learn to notice your immediate gut response when the request is made. This can be an infallible guide as to whether or not you really want to say 'Yes' or 'No' in reply.

2. If you hesitate, ask for more information about what you commitment would entail if you were to agree to the request.

3. Remember you have a right to say 'No' for yourself. When you say 'Yes' and deny your wish to say 'No', you put yourself down and deny your own importance. You will also find a way of saying 'No' indirectly.

4. Practise saying 'No' clearly and directly, without excessive apology or justification.

5. Whenever possible, take responsibility for saying 'No' rather than blaming someone else as an excuse.

6. Remember, you are refusing the request, not rejecting the person.

7. Saying 'No' and surviving the awful guilt gets easier with practice!

Bill of Personal Rights

Each person should draw up their own bill of personal rights. The one that follows is an example, but each individual may have different wants and needs.

---

1. I have the right not be perfect and the right to make mistakes

2. I have the right to be treated with respect as an equal human being

3. I have the right to change my mind

4. I have the right to express my own opinions, feelings and values

5. I have the right to ask for what I want

6. I have the right to decline responsibility for other people's problems and bad behaviour

7. I have the right to protest against unfair criticism or treatment

8. I have the right to say no

9. I have the right to do things in my own way without seeking the approval of others

10. I have the right to ask for more time to consider before making a decision

---

Now work out what your own personal charter is. If you can only come up with two or three personal rights, you need self-assertiveness training.

Once you have drawn it up, type it or write it out neatly, and have it framed. Hang it in a prominent place – in the kitchen, or the lounge, somewhere where you will see it several times a day. Read it out loud, memorise it, believe it. Have it in the front of your mind in any situation, and act on it.

When you accept that you have personal rights you no longer feel guilty about being self-assertive. For example:

A young mother has decided to return to work and contacts a baby minder who agrees to look after her children. On leaving the woman's house she is aware of a gut feeling telling her this woman is not the right person to care for her children, and she wants to cancel the arrangement.

If she is self-assertive she will telephone the woman as soon as she gets home, thank her for offering to take on the job of baby minding but say she has changed her mind and does not want to employ her.

If she is not self-assertive she may:

● Find someone else to do the job, just not contact the first woman again, and feel guilty; or

● Lie to the woman, saying she has decided not to go back to work after all, and feel guilty; or

● Take the children to this woman and discover they are not happy and the arrangement is not working, thus creating problems in the future.

She has the right to change her mind

A husband gets home from work and his wife tells him the car has been damaged by someone backing into it in the car park.

He hits the roof. 'You're a hopeless driver, you're always smashing up the car', he yells.

If she is assertive she will say, 'Will you stop shouting at me and tell me when I have been responsible for damaging the car in the past? The other driver has admitted it was his fault and has agreed to pay for the damage.'

She has the right to protest against unfair criticism

The self-assertive person is much easier to get on with in the long run than the passive person because they know what they want and what they will not accept. They can communicate this to those they come into contact with, and everyone knows where they stand. Life becomes much simpler all round.

If you say 'No' you must mean 'No' and show you mean it. If you assert your rights you must follow the assertion through. For example:

A mother tells her child next time he hits his baby sister he will be sent to his room. The child does it again, but the mother is busy and does not carry out the threat. The child does not understand that the mother really means what she said and that he must not hit his sister; he is confused.

It is important to be consistent in what you say and assert. But just saying what you mean is not enough if your body language does not support your words. If you believe in what you are saying you must delive your statement with confidence. Eye contact is an important way of giving weight to your words. If you are telling someone something they don't want to hear, looking them straight in the eye shows you mean business, and that they'll just have to lump it!

LOOKING AFTER YOURSELF

Looking after yourself means paying attention to:

● Diet, including alcohol intake

● Exercise

● Coping with stress

● Getting adequate sleep

Diet

With regard to general eating habits, as far as possible you should:

● Eat fresh fruit and vegetables daily

● Include sufficient fibre

● Avoid fried and fatty foods

● Not eat too many refined foods

● Make meals interesting and get variety and colour into your food

● Find time to sit down, relax and enjoy your meals

● Not become obsessive about what you can and can't eat

● Aim for a sensible balanced diet

Low Blood Sugar

Some people with eating problems, alcoholics, drug addicts and others suffer from low blood sugar levels. Intake of sugary food, caffeine and alcohol causes a rapid raising of the blood sugar level. The pancreas responds by producing insulin to convert the sugar into usable energy and even a tired body gets a temporary lift. However when the sugar is used up there may be an excess of insulin left over in the system, so blood sugar levels fall, giving a condition called hypoglaecemia. As blood sugar levels are dropping some of the symptoms that may appear include:

Food cravings

Coffee craving

Alcohol craving

Tobacco craving

Tiredness

Irritability

Depression

Lack of concentration

Headaches

Shaky hands

If this fluctuation between high and low levels becomes an habitual way of life it can wear down the pancreas, causing it to act less efficiently, thus perpetuating the problem. To stabilise blood sugar levels it is important to eat regularly and include at least 90 grammes of protein a day in the diet. Don't go more than three to four hours without eating a snack or meal containing protein. Cut out sugary foods, refined foods (such as white flour, processed packet foods), caffeine (coffee, tea, cocoa, cola), and alcohol.

Overweight

Avoid crash diets or very low calorie diets, they are doomed to failure in the long run. Make permanent changes in your eating style. Substitute fresh fruit and vegetables for sugary and fried foods. Aim to lose not more than 2 lb a week and set yourself a realistic goal weight. Never put off doing things because you are overweight. If you have an eating disorder seek professional help.

Alcohol

A small amount of alcohol, which means a glass of wine, half a pint of beer or a tot of whisky, daily can be relaxing and beneficial, but if alcohol is a problem it is best to give it up completely. Anyone with an eating problem should keep off alcohol until their eating is well under control.

The following questions (based on a London Council on Alcoholism questionnaire) are designed to help you assess your drinking habits and find out whether you have a problem with alcohol, and how serious that problem is.

In each question, tick the statement which is true, or closest to the truth, for you – one tick for each position. Then add up your score as shown below.

1. If I was advised to give up drinking for health reasons:

    (a) I could do so easily

    (b) I could do so but I'd miss it

    (c) I could do so but with difficulty

    (d) I could only do so if I had help

    (e) I don't think I could do it

2. This time last year my favourite drink was:

    (a) stronger than what I drink now

    (b) weaker than what I drink now

(c) the same as what I drink now

3. When I am drinking with my friends I notice that:

   (a) they seem to drink about the same speed that I do

   (b) they drink faster than I do

   (c) some of them drink more slowly than I do

   (d) most of them drink more slowly than I do

If you answered yes to (a) or (b) also answer the following:

My new friends:

   (e) drink faster than my old friends

   (f) drink slower than my old friends

4. Where I buy my drink:

   (a) I have a credit account

   (b) I do not have a credit account

If you answered yes to (a), then also answer the following:

The amount that I owe on my credit account is:

   (c) generally about what I would expect

   (d) sometimes rather more than I'd expected

5. I usually first think about drinking:

   (a) when I wake up

   (b) some time during the morning

(c) at lunchtime

(d) late in the afternoon

(e) in the evening

If you answered yes to (a), (b), or (c) then also answer the following:

When I plan the rest of my day:

(f) drinking is a high priority

(g) drinking is not particularly important to me

6. Before going to a social event:

(a) I never have a drink

(b) I seldom have a drink

(c) I usually have a drink

7. When I decide whether to go to a social event:

(a) it doesn't matter to me whether or not alcohol is going to be available there

(b) I prefer some drink to be available there

(c) I don't really enjoy it unless some drink is going to be available

(d) I will only attend if I know drink will be available there

8. After I have had a few drinks:

(a) I never pretend to have had less than I really have

(b) I occasionally do pretend that

(c) I often do pretend that

(d) I sometimes declare I had one more drink then I've actually had

9. When it gets towards closing time:

(a) I find I've had enough to drink

(b) I tend to double my final order or buy some to take home with me

10. In the course of everyday conversation my friends:

(a) seldom talk about drinking

(b) quite often talk about drinking

If you answered yes to (b) then also answer the following:

I have noticed that my friends usually:

(c) joke about it

(d) offer some kind of advice to me

(e) talk about drinking much more than me

Add up your score as follows and then assess yourself according to the following 'categories':

1.	a = 1, b = 1, c = 2, d = 3, e = 4
2.	a = 1, b = 3, c = 2
3.	a = 1, b = 1, c = 2, d = 3, e = 4, f = 2
4.	a = 2, b = 1, c = 1, d = 2
5.	a = 4, b = 3, c = 2, d = 1, e = 1, f = 3, g = 1
6.	a = 1, b = 2, c = 3
7.	a = 1, b = 2, c = 3, d = 4
8.	a = 1, b = 3, c = 4, d = 2
9.	a = 1, b = 3
10.	a = 1, b = 2, c = 3, d = 4, e = 1

Relax: If you scored 17 or under you are not a dependent drinker and have no need to worry at present about your drinking habits. But don't forget that drinking habits can change, particularly in times of stress, and you may not *stay* a non-dependent drinker.

Be wary: If you scored from 18 to 24 you are probably a regular, but moderate drinker. You may feel a 'need' to drink now and then, and may be causing yourself harm – or causing others difficulties – from time to time.

You are in the area of mildly vulnerable drinking, and should watch your consumption carefully for signs of drinking more, or more often. If your friends say that you are starting to drink more, take heed: remember that it is very easy to move along towards the problem end of drinking.

Cut down: If you scored 25 to 30, you are probably drinking regularly and drinking too much for the good of your health and relationships. You may not notice the 'need' to drink – because you rarely go without it. You are now running a very high risk of developing more serious drink problems, so try to cut down the amount you drink, and to drink less often.

Seek help: If you scored over 31 you are probably dependent, physically and psychologically, on alcohol. You are certainly harming yourself and could be causing suffering to others.

If you stop drinking or try to cut down you may experience unpleasant withdrawal symptoms (trembling, sweating, feelings of panic), and may feel confused, moody or depressed. As time goes on you will need more and more alcohol to reach the same level of intoxication. You should seek professional help.

Smoking

Statistics prove that smoking vastly increase the risk of serious illness such as lung disease and heart disease. Nicotine is an addictive drug and giving up the smoking habit is not easy. Because it can be extremely difficult, stressful and even traumatic to give up smoking, you should not try to do it while you are also working on getting over an eating, drink or drug problem or are in some particularly stressful situation. It is important to get to the root of why you smoke and be ready to cope with the challenge of giving up. When you feel the time has come to give up, a recommended way is to use Nicorette chewing gum which your doctor can prescribe. Combine this with relaxation or meditation exercises.

Exercise

Everybody needs exercise. It combats stress, tones you up, clears the mind and makes you feel good. Find a form of exercise that you enjoy and that suits your level of health and fitness. Don't do something you don't like just because it is fashionable or because other people urge you to do it. Exercise could be taking the dog for a walk, playing a round of golf, or running a marathon. Alternatively you could abandon the car and ride a bicycle to work, or walk up the stairs instead of using the lift. Swimming is an activity that suits nearly everybody, especially those with health problems and disabilities that make other forms of exercise difficult, such as arthritis, heart disease and overweight.

Stress

A certain amount of stress is good for us, it's what keeps us going.

It's when it becomes 'distress' that it is a problem. The following questions are designed to help you assess whether you are currently suffering from stress.

1. Is stress currently affecting you physically?

For each question, tick the category of answer, (a), (b), or (c), which most closely applies to you.

	(a)	(b)	(c)
	Once a week or more often	Once a month	Less than once a month (or not at all)

Is your sleep disturbed by any of the following:

(a) difficulty in getting to sleep			
(b) waking frequently in the night			
(c) waking in the early hours, unable to sleep again			
Are you experiencing sexual difficulties? (impotence, lack of desire for sex, etc.)			
Do you have difficulty in sitting still without fidgeting?			
Do you have headaches?			
Do you bite your nails?			
Do you feel unusually tired?			
Do you have frequent indigestion such as heartburn?			
Do you crave for food other than at mealtimes?			
Do you have no appetite at mealtimes?			
Is bowel function erratic–sometimes constipated, sometimes very loose?			
Do you sweat for no obvious reason?			
Do you have an 'tics' such as touching your face, hair, moustache, etc repeatedly?			
Do you frequently feel sick or queasy?			
Do you ever faint or have dizzy spells without obvious cause?			
Do you feel breathless and tight-chested when not exerting yourself?			
Do you cry or feel you want to cry?			
Are you suffering from high blood pressure?			
Do you feel obliged to have a drink to 'unwind'?			
Do you smoke to calm your nerves?			

If you ticked (a) for two or more of these questions (two (b) ticks equal one (a) tick) then, almost certainly, your body is reacting to stress, and it is time to do something about it.

2. Is stress currently affecting you mentally?

	(a) Once a week or more often	(b) Once a month	(c) Less than once a month (or not at all)
Do you lack interest in life?			
Do you feel helpless and unable to cope?			
Are you irritable without obvious cause?			
Are your frequently aware of being afraid of disease?			
Do you feel yourself to be a failure?			
Do you dislike yourself?			
Do you have difficulty making up your mind?			
Are you uninterested in other people?			
Is it difficult to show your true feelings?			
Do you feel suppressed (i.e. unexpressed) anger?			
Do you feel your appearance has altered for the worse?			
Do you find it difficult to relax and laugh?			
Do you feel that other people dislike you?			
Do you feel you are neglected, or have been let down?			
Do you feel you have 'failed' in your role as parents, spouse, child?			
Do you have a fear of what the future holds?			
Do you feel no one understands you?			
Do you feel isolated and that there is no one to turn to?			
Do you find it difficult to concentrate?			

Do you find it difficult to complete one job properly before rushing on to the next?

Do you fear enclosed or open spaces?

Do you feel uncomfortable in touching and being touched?

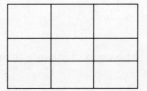

If you ticked (a) for three or more of these questions (two (b) ticks equal one (a) tick), probably then you are emotionally affected by stress. See these signs as a warning and a challenge to be met by personal effort. If on this and the previous list, a combined total of five or more (a) answers were given, then it might be advisable to seek professional advice.

Anxiety Tendency Check-list

You may have had low scores on the previous check-lists, and yet have a tendency towards future problems. The following chart was designed by Dr Charles Spielberger, Professor of Psychology at the University of South Florida, as a means of evaluating your own tendency towards anxiety.

'Read each statement and then circle the appropriate number that indicates how you generally feel. There are no right or wrong answers. Do not spend too much time on any one statement, but give the answer which seems to describe how you generally feel. Add up the eight numbers you have circled to obtain your score.

	Almost never	Sometimes	Often	Almost always
I feel nervous and restless	1	2	3	4
I feel satisfied with myself	4	3	2	1
I feel that difficulties are piling up so that I cannot overcome them	1	2	3	4
I feel a failure	1	2	3	4

	Almost never	Sometimes	Often	Almost always
I have disturbing thoughts	1	2	3	4
I lack self-confidence	1	2	3	4
I feel secure	4	3	2	1
I worry too much over something that really does not matter	1	2	3	4

Only five per cent of the population has a score of ten or less. Half the population has a score of around fifteen. Only five per cent of the population has a score of over twenty.'

Statistics can mislead, but the point is that if you are scoring over fifteen, you are definitely too stressed, and you should do something about it.

What to do about stress

● Don't work more than 10 hours a day, whether at home and or work.

● Take at least one good break during the working day. Take at least a day and a half off a week. Take an annual holiday away from your usual environment.

● Don't feel embarrassed about seeking professional help with any emotional or sexual problems that are causing distress. There are self-help organisations for almost all problems and diseases; there is nothing wrong in asking for help for yourself or others.

● Don't overspend, get into debt or commit yourself to more than you can afford. If you get into financial trouble seek out help from your Bank, Building Society or the Citizens' Advice Bureau.

- Avoid over-committing yourself to others and yourself. Allow yourself time to relax and enjoy a breathing space.

- If you are worried about your health, go and see your doctor and tell him how you really feel. He can't help you if you are not honest with him.

- Stop worrying about what you assume others might be thinking about you: your assumption may well be wrong anyway.

- Don't try to do too many things at the same time. If you are not a naturally well-organised person, make a list and schedules to guide you, but don't become ruled by them.

- Exercise regularly, at least two or three times a week. Choose a form of exercise you enjoy and which is suited to your health and personal fitness.

- Meditation classes are held at many evening institutes, health centres and hospitals. It is nothing to do with religion but a natural way to relax and get in touch with yourself.

- Yoga combines relaxation and meditation with exercise that is non-competitive. Relaxation tapes are useful to play at home. The Alexander Technique teaches posture and body awareness.

- Caffeine, found in coffee, tea, cocoa and cola, is a stimulant. Try to cut down or eliminate it. Drink decaffeinated coffee as an alternative.

- Alcohol should not be taken as an anti-stress measure.

- Have a good laugh. Go to see a funny film, read an amusing book, seek out people with a good sense of humour.

- Get enough sleep.

Sleep

Everyone has different sleep requirements. The quality of sleep is probably more important than the quantity. Too much sleep can make you tired, as can too little. Not everybody needs eight hours. To improve the quality of your sleep:

1. Cut down or eliminate caffeine.

2. Wind down and relax before you go to bed. Warm milk is a relaxing bedtime drink.

3. Make sure you have some fresh air and exercise during the day.

4. If you have a lot of worries or things on your mind, write them down before you go to bed and put the list aside until tomorrow.

5. Don't worry about not sleeping; you don't die from lack of sleep. If you do wake in the night it may be better to get up, have a warm drink, and read for a while rather than lie in bed worrying.

6. Don't let the sun go down on your anger. If you can't sort out your differences in person, write a letter; you don't have to post it.

7. Make sure the room is not too hot or too cold and the bed is comfortable.

8. Make sure you have not overeaten late at night, nor are you hungry.

Don't resort to sleeping tablets: they are addictive and have side-effects. The sleep they produce is unnatural and of poor quality. After two or three weeks they lose their effectiveness but by then you are addicted to them. A good alternative to sleeping tablets would be L-Tryptophan, an amino-acid which is used by the body to produce a brain chemical important for inducing relaxation and sleep. It has no side-effects and is non-addictive. It can be acquired either on prescription from the doctor or at health food shops.

Checklist: Are you looking after yourself?

	Yes	Sometimes	No
Do you work more than $5^1/_2$ days weekly?			
Do you work more than 10 hours on a work day?			
Do you take less than half an hour for each main meal?			
Do you eat quickly and not chew thoroughly?			
Do you smoke?			
Do you get less than seven hours' sleep daily?			
Do you listen to relaxing music?			
Do you practise daily relaxation or meditation?			
Do you take 30 minutes exercise at least three times weekly?			
Do you have a creative hobby (gardening, painting, needlework, etc)?			
Do you play any non-competitive sport (walking, swimming, cycling), or belong to a yoga or exercise class?			
Do you try to have a siesta or short rest period during the day?			
Do you have regular massage or osteopathic attention?			
Do you spend at least half an hour outdoors in daylight each day?			

The first six answers should all be 'No'. (Two 'sometimes' answer equal one 'Yes'.) All 'Yes' answers here show you need to make some lifestyle changes. The answers to the following questions should be 'Yes'. (Two 'Sometimes' answers equal one 'No'.) All 'No' answers here show a need for changes.

Look at this chart again in six months' time. If you have really started looking after yourself, you'll be ticking the right answers!

DEPRESSION

There are several different types of depression. It is a vast subject covering many symptoms and degrees of suffering.

Reactive depression: the consequence of some trauma such as bereavement, loss of job, divorce. Counselling is helpful in coming to terms with the situation. There is nothing shameful in seeking professional help.

Endogenous depression: appears for no apparent reason, characterised by total despair helplessness and a great sense of unworthiness. Many people with eating problems suffer from this. Anti-depressants may help for a short period in extreme cases, but after that they only cloud the mind and may prevent the sufferer seeking the appropriate professional help.

Hormonal depression: post-natal, pre-menstrual tension and menopausal.

Manic depression: needs medical treatment.

There are different degrees of depression. In extreme cases with suicidal feelings it is important to receive professional help. Mild depression, which shares many of the symptoms of stress, is like living constantly under a black cloud, there is no joy in life. There is a lot you can do to help yourself out of this state.

Drugs will not cure the root cause of the depression. They can clear your mind sufficiently to put you in a position to help yourself, but there is no point in carrying on with repeat prescriptions. Therapy and self-help are needed.

L-Tryptophan, as mentioned previously, is to be recommended as it is beneficial in many cases.

There are many different types of therapy and many kinds of therapists; your doctor will recommend one. If you don't get on with one person, ask for a referral.

Probably as useful are seminars and workshops on specific problems such as self-esteem, self-assertiveness, and communication.

Pre-menstrual tension (PMT)

In severe cases of PMT a doctor or clinic can prescribe hormone replacement therapy. In milder cases:

● Get more rest

● Avoid stress at that time of the month

● Take Vitamin B6 and Oil of Evening Primrose

● Take extra care with diet in the pre-menstrual period

Post-natal depression

'Baby blues' in the first few days after the birth are very common and usually disappear quite soon. Longer lasting and deeper depression needs medical attention, and this should be sought urgently if symptoms of aggression towards the baby develop.

Menopausal depression

The two causes of depression at this stage of life can often be interlinked. One cause is hormonal and this can be helped with hormone replacement therapy. The other cause is psychological. Some women see the change of life as signalling the end of their usefulness and it strikes deeply at the roots of their identity as a woman, wife and mother. It may also be a reminder that life is passing them by. However, it should be viewed as an opportunity to begin a new and fulfilling phase of life.

Are you depressed?

How often do these thoughts go through your mind:

● I'm useless

● I'm guilty

- I can't cope

- Nobody likes me

- I don't like myself

- I am a failure

- Things will never get better

- I've got no friends

- I'm bored

- I've got no money

- I'm fat

- I'm ugly

- People tease me

- I'm always tired

- I can't concentrate

- I'm lonely

- I'll feel better if I have a drink

- I'm never lucky

- I've forgotten how to laugh

- I wish I was dead

- Nobody would miss me if I was dead

- Everybody's better off than me

● I'm not a good mother

● I've had no proper education

● I dread the weekends

● I hate Christmas

● Everybody else is going on holiday

● ..... and they've got someone to go with

● I'm a victim

● My parents don't understand me

These are all negative assumptions. Each one has a positive side. For example:

'Nobody likes me'

First take out the assumption: make it into a realistic statement – you don't *know* everybody.

It is impossible to be liked by everybody.

Ask a question:

'What can I do to be liked by the few people that matter to me?'

'I am a victim'

Write down when you were last a victim.

– I had my purse stolen recently, for the third time.

How did you set yourself up to be a victim?

– I did not close my handbag, and put it down in a crowded place.

What will you do to change things in the future?

– I will always keep my handbag shut and be more aware of security.

'I feel guilty'

What makes you feel guilty?

– I shout at my children and don't do the housework

The belief is: good people don't get angry and good wives keep the house clean at all times.

Change the action:

– don't lose your temper, and do more housework

or

Change the belief:

– I am a good person. Sometimes good people lose their temper, and they don't keep their house tidy all the time.

Self-help

There are many things you can do for yourself to help relieve the symptoms of depression. For example:

● Get enough sleep

● Take up an interesting hobby

● Don't sit at home, go to work, college, get out of the house at least part of the day

● Don't spend too much time alone

● Join a self-help group for people who are suffering from

depression so you can work on your problems together. A lot of places have day centres

- Take plenty of exercise

- Don't dwell on the past

- Learn to cope with stress

- Take an interest in other people

- Write down what is making you depressed, try to get it straight in your mind, then do something about it.

- Attitude is all-important. A positive attitude is essential

- Make a note of your successes, however small

- Make a chart so you can see what you have achieved

- Take an interest in your appearance and in your surroundings. Wear bright colours, have fresh flowers in the house. Don't sit in a gloomy room with curtains drawn. If the sun is out, let it shine on you.

The majority of people suffer from some form of depression at some stage in their life. At the time it seems there is no way out, a dark cloud totally envelops you and the future does not exist. However, you can dispel that cloud and put depression behind you for the rest of your life *if you choose to do so*. Then you can look back on it as just one more chapter in your life, a chapter from which you learnt a lot about yourself and about life, and which has enhanced the quality of your living today.

BOREDOM

The word 'to bore' in the context of meaning 'to weary or annoy with tediousness' was unknown in the English language before the 18th century. That is not to say that bordeom didn't exist 300 years ago, but in the late 20th century it has grown into a problem that is reaching epidemic proportions.

Television must shoulder much of the blame for this. It offers instant entertainment, 24 hours a day 'companionship', the maximum colour, sound and action for the minimum effort. Nearly every home has at least one TV set and nearly every viewer must admit, if they are honest, to sitting in front of programmes they do not enjoy out of the sheer inertia. When television starts to take over it becomes dangerous. Families lose the skill of communication, individuals forget or never learn how to be creative and how to spend time in satisfying and fulfilling occupations.

Despite the pace of modern life it is too easy to do nothing. Even the person who is 'busy' all day long can be bored with life if no aspect of that activity is satisfying or fulfilling. Housework has to be done, livings have to be earned, and those who find total satisfaction in these things alone will not be bored. But most people need something more in their life – hobbies, stimulating company, ambitions, achievements – to give the day a lift. We need something to look forward to on waking and to reflect on with satisfaction on going to sleep at night. A day that achieves nothing is a wasted day. But even the smallest achievement, something that gives that little glow of inner pleasure, makes the day worth while.

Assessing your boredom level

How bored are you? At what level do you live an average day? Fill in a graph like the one overleaf to see it in black and white in front of you.

Mark your mood at each point in an average day, then join the marks to give a picture of your lifestyle. The illustration shows one person dragging along in a joyless existence, another leading an enjoyable and satisfying life.

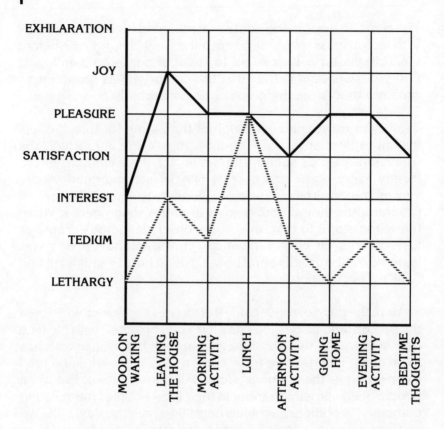

1. The person represented by the dotted line wakes up tired, thinking 'Not another day'. By the time she is dressed and out of the house she starts to feel a bit better. Reading the paper passes the journey to the office. Work is tedious and boring, this person can't wait for lunch, the only bright spot of the day. More tedious work, and by the end of the day she feel exhausted going home to an empty house and a load of dirty dishes. She watches TV all evening, flopped out in front of an uninteresting programme, goes to bed tired, does not look forward to tomorrow, and may even dread it.

2. The person represented by the solid line wakes up looking forward to the day, goes for an early morning walk with the dog and chats with neighbours. This person has an interesting and challenging job, she enjoys a healthy lunch in good

company and feels satisfied with a day's work. It is a pleasure to return to a homely flat and a welcome from the dog, then it is out to an evening class on computer skills which she sees as an enjoyable way of learning something new with a view to future promotion at work. This is followed by a meal with classmates, then home for a late night stroll with the dog, a warm bath and bed, well satisfied with life.

A lot of people do not realise they are bored. They are stuck in a rut, doing things out of habit without really enjoying them, not aware how many changes could make life more fulfilling. Fill in the following questionnaire and study it to discover how much of your life you find enjoyable and fulfilling.

	Yesterday	In the past week
1. How many TV programmes did you watch for the sake of having it on or because it was easier than doing something else?		
2. How many programmes did you find interesting and stimulating?		
3. How many hours did you spend on hobbies you enjoy?		
4. How many hours did you spend entertaining? Add your pleasure rating on a scale of 1–10.		
5. How many hours did you spend meeting others or visiting? Add pleasure rating 1–10.		
6. How many hours did you spend visiting pub/cinema/restaurant/clubs /class? Add pleasure rating 1–10.		

	Yesterday	In the past week
7. How many hours did you spend reading something new, interesting and stimulating?		
8. How many hours did you spend talking to somebody interesting and stimulating?		
9. How many hours did you spend on unnecessary chores and drudgery?		
10. How many hours did you spend in a job that bores you to tears?		

If you are a bored person you are probably also a boring person. What have you got to offer in a relationship? Ask yourself:

1. How many topics of conversation do you have?

2. How many subjects are you interested in, other than yourself?

3. Are you prepared to try taking an interest in or participating in something you know nothing about?

If your are a bored person you are probably too lethargic to do anything about making life more interesting. Ask yourself:

1. How much interest do you actually take in your work and the company you work for?

2. Have you asked to be given more interesting work?

3. Have you looked for a more interesting job?

4. Have you considered getting more qualifications so you can

get a better job?

5. If you are unemployed, what steps are you taking to get another job, retrain, take a job that isn't exactly what you want, do voluntary work?

6. Are you lethargic because you are bored, or are you bored because you are fatigued?

7. Do you drink and/or binge eat because you are bored?

8. What hobbies would you like to take up that you haven't?

9. Why haven't you taken up these hobbies:

   (a) no money

   (b) no time

   (c) no confidence

   (d) spouse wouldn't like it

   (e) other

SELF-DECEPTION

So many people with eating disorders are victims of their own self-deception. One very common form of this is the 'Everything will be all right once I'm slim' attitude, the belief that life will change miraculously when the desired weight is achieved. But have you ever asked yourself how different your life would *really* be if you weighed a few pounds less?

If you are within half a stone of your ideal weight, try answering the following questions:

1. How did you decide what your ideal weight is?

2. Did you look at a number of charts or just one? ('Ideal weights' can vary by up to a stone.)

3. Is your ideal weight less than that generally given by charts because you want to allow yourself room for bingeing, special occasions like Christmas or holidays, etc?

4. What difference would it make to your life if you were at your ideal weight?

5. Will your children/husband/parents/boy-friend love you more if you weigh a few pounds less?

6. Would your job be less boring if you weighed a few pounds less?

7. Do you think your everyday chores would become less tedious if you did not have to worry about your weight?

8. Do you think that if you weighed a few pounds less the ideal job/partner would come along?

9. Do you think your financial situation would improve?

10. Do you think you would be less lonely if you weighed slightly less?

11. Do you think your boss would treat you better?

12. Do you think losing a few pounds would prevent a member of your family from becoming ill?

13. Do you think you would find your school/university/work easier if you weighed less?

Write down the answers–and then look at them again in six months' time and see whether your attitude has changed.

Taking down the barriers

Many people with eating disorders (or drink or drug problems) put up barriers and hide behind 'I can't', without really asking themselves '**Why** can't I?'.

What are your aims, your immediate 'wants in life? What lifestyle changes do you want to make – and what blocks have you put up to prevent you from achieving your wants?

Start being honest with yourself. Decide on what you want, and then examine what is stopping you from getting it.

Write down your wants on a blank sheet of paper. They don't have to be earth-shattering – they do have to be realistic. The following is an example.

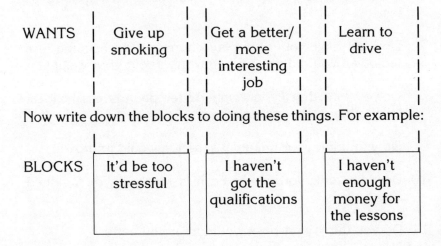

WANTS	Give up smoking	Get a better/ more interesting job	Learn to drive

Now write down the blocks to doing these things. For example:

BLOCKS	It'd be too stressful	I haven't got the qualifications	I haven't enough money for the lessons

Now examine each one in turn. Try to find a solution that will knock down that block you've put up. For example:

1.

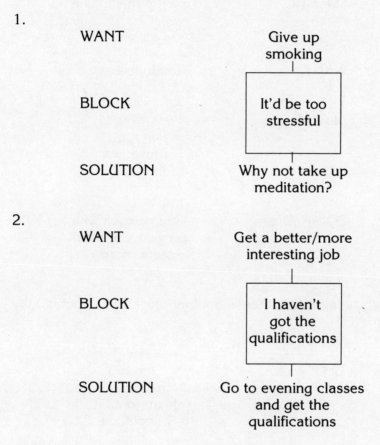

WANT	Give up smoking
BLOCK	It'd be too stressful
SOLUTION	Why not take up meditation?

2.

WANT	Get a better/more interesting job
BLOCK	I haven't got the qualifications
SOLUTION	Go to evening classes and get the qualifications

Now you may well find yourself putting up more blocks to the solution, eg:

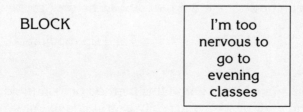

BLOCK   I'm too nervous to go to evening classes

So work through this block, too:

SOLUTION   Take up meditation

3.

WANT   Learn to drive

BLOCK

| I haven't enough money for the lessons |

SOLUTION   Your new job will provide you with more money

Now you realise that there's another block hiding behind the first one:

BLOCK

| I'm too nervous to learn to drive; I couldn't do it |

So you can now tackle the real block, the root problem:

SOLUTION   Take up meditation

Time and again I have found this method of writing down your wants and their blocks, and really examining them, works with my clients. Once you have been honest with yourself, once you have discovered the real root problem, and tackled that, you can work your way back through the other blocks – and you are well on your way to achieving your aims.

MOTIVATION

If you are stuck in a negative image of yourself and are convinced you are a failure you will not be motivated to try to make improvements. Having read this far, though, you will, hopefully, have realised the importance of raising your self esteem, and of seeing yourself in a positive way. The motivation may already be stirring within you to make improvements.

The following exercises will provide steps on that road to improvement. The examples given are for someone with an eating problem, but they can just as easily be used to help overcome a drink or a drugs problem.

Exercise 1

When you wake up in the morning say to yourself: 'Just for today, I am not going to binge' as 'just for today I am not going to weigh myself; as 'just for today I am going to eat regular meals'.

Whichever of these you choose for the day, keep saying it to yourself and write it down at least once every half hour. Just for today: tomorrow will have a new challenge, this is your battle for today.

Exercise 2

When you feel the urge to eat something you know you shouldn't: stop.

Press the tip of each thumb against the side of the index finger of the same hand, just by the base of the nail, and hold the point firmly.

Take a deep breath.

Continue breathing slowly and deeply while you count slowly to ten. Deep slow breathing helps you to concentrate on relaxing. You were probably starting to breathe quickly at the thought of eating.

If you still feel agitated repeat the slow breathing while you count to ten again.

Now consider calmly and rationally whether you really need to eat just at this moment. Could you not put it off for half an hour?

If you succeed in delaying your eating for just half an hour, you have had a success – and it might motivate you to extend that time until you reach a proper meal, but don't expect to succeed every time. Let failure be the motivation to succeed next time.

Exercise 3

Take a large sheet of blank paper and rule a line down the centre. On the left-hand side of the page, write a positive statement that you feel is relevant to your particular problem, addressing yourself by name, followed by 'because ....' Then on the right hand side of the page, write down the first reason that comes into your head. When you have done this, return to the left-hand column and repeat your original statement, followed by 'because ......', then on the right put down the next reason that comes into your head. Continue until you run out of reasons. It is important to repeat this exercise at the same time each day. At the end of the week, read through your answers and see what you have learnt from them. Your page might look something like this:

I, Jane Smith, don't eat chocolate biscuits because ...	They make me fat:
I, Jane Smith, don't eat chocolate biscuits because ...	I know if I eat one, I will eat the whole packet.

Cop-outs

There are always plenty of very good reasons for *not* doing something. Excuses pop up so easily when you feel you can't be bothered and are not motivated. Some of the most popular excuses are listed below, but listen to yourself and write your own list.

- It will sort itself out if I do nothing

- It's an unpleasant job

- Tomorrow will do just as well,

- It's too late in the day, I'll wait till tomorrow

- I don't have the right equipment/papers/etc.

- It's difficult, I don't think I can do it

- It's not urgent, I'll do it later

- It might hurt

- If I leave it someone else might do it for me

- It might cause me embarrassment

- I don't know where to start

- I'm too tired

- It's a boring chore

- It's a waste of time because it probably wouldn't work

- I've got to tidy up first

- I want to watch this TV programme

- It's no good starting now, I'll be interrupted

- The weather's too nice to spend the day indoors

- It's too late now

- Before I start I'll ...
                    take a break

have a coffee

have a cigarette

have a few biscuits

How valid are your excuses?

If there is something you feel you ought to do or would like to do but are just not motivated, and don't get round to doing, try writing down a comparison of the advantages and disadvantages of the action, which should clarify your ideas and help you to come to logical conclusions about how to overcome your negative attitude. An example is given in the following chart:

Example

You quite like the idea of signing up for an evening class in yoga, but can't get round to filling in the application form.

ADVANTAGES	DISADVANTAGES	LOGICAL THINKING
It would get me out in the evenings.	I would have to take the car out on frosty winter nights.	I am a competent driver and have often driven in bad conditions. On really bad nights I can call a taxi. I can go with someone else who is prepared to drive.
I would meet new people.	If nobody speaks to me I will feel unhappy and rejected.	It is up to me to speak to others and be friendly and approachable.
I would learn to relax and would feel better for the exercise.	I can't stand on my head and twist my legs up in knots so I would look a fool in front of the rest of the class.	I am going to join a beginners' class so nobody will be any better than me. Yoga is totally non-competitive and the others will be too busy concentrating on themselves to notice what I am doing.

Forward planning

It is very easy to forget that you wanted to do something. You get carried away by activities of the moment, and good intentions slip your mind. By forward planning you can be prepared. When you have an idea for doing something, make yourself reminders. For example:

1. While driving home you spot an interesting footpath and intend to explore where it goes one day.

   BUT

   On the following Sunday afternoon you have nothing to do and can't think of anywhere to go. You have forgotten you wanted to go on that walk so you sit at home and watch TV. A note about the footpath in a prominent place, i.e. on top of the television, would have reminded you.

2. You think it would be a nice idea to go for an early swim tomorrow.

   BUT

   You get up next morning, wash, dress, put on your make-up, have breakfast then remember the swim – but it is too late ... If you had got out your swimsuit and towel the night before and left them in the bathroom, you would have remembered when you got up.

Getting motivated

Learn to recognise negative thinking and work out the positive side of each thought. For example:

Negative	*Positive*
I can't stick to an eating plan	I haven't up until now, but there is no reason why I shouldn't in the future.
I don't enjoy anything	I enjoy things when I feel good. If I do something I will probably enjoy it when I get started.

My hair is such a mess, I can't go out.	I can wash it tonight and make an appointment at the hairdresser's for tomorrow.
I don't have time to do anything I enjoy	I don't have to clean the whole house every day. I deserve some time for myself each day. I don't need to be at everyone's beck and call all the time.
I'm too fat to do anything	Being fat does not stop me going to the theatre, walking the dog, reading an interesting book or doing an Open University Degree.

● Just take one small step to begin with. Often just doing one small thing will provide motivation to carry on. Don't try to make huge changes all at once.

● Each night when you go to bed write down a list of your achievements, however small, during the day and how you felt about each one. Make a schedule for the coming day.

● Motivation is doing something.

EPILOGUE

The root of my philosophy is summed up like this:

- Everyone has a choice in every situation. It is your choice where you stop the elevator – you are the only one who can push the button to half the downward journey, and it is your choice when you push it.

IT'S UP TO YOU

- Learn to like yourself and take care of yourself.

- Communicate. It's vital in any relationship.

- Become more self-assertive.

- Don't give in to boredom, seek out self-fulfilment.

- Improve your self-esteem.

- Recognise stress and deal with it in an appropriate manner.

- Improve the quality of your life in these ways, and depression will lift.

Once you have mastered all that you will be well on the way to a satisfactory lifestyle. It is the road I am aiming to take in the years ahead and the route I shall be pointing out to many, many more clients with eating problems. I don't see the epidemic of addiction and compulsive behaviour fading away in the foreseeable future, in fact I think it will grow and touch even more people as the world races along, sweeping us all up in the stress and pace of modern life.

A few may choose to go and sit in the penthouse meditating on love and peace. The rest of us somehow have to carry on in the teeming world below, plodding upwards and drifting downwards as we shape the course of our lives. We all need to learn how to survive in an appropriate manner.
Remember, life is not a rehearsal–go for it now!

RECOMMENDED READING LIST

Book	Author	Publisher	Date of Publication
The Food Trap	Paulette Maisner with Rosemary Turner	Unwin Hyman Ltd	1985
Excuses Won't Cure You	Paulette Maisner with Alison Cridland	Unwin Hyman Ltd	1987
Feeling Good	David D. Burns M.D.	Signet	1981
Depression	Dr Caroline Shreeve	Thorsons	1984
Men Who Hate Women and the Women Who Love Them	Dr Susan Forward	Bantam	1986
Feel the Fear and Do it Anyway	Susan Jeffers	Century	1987
Stress-Proving Programme	Leon Chaitow ND.DO. MBNOA	Thorsons	1985
Doing it Now	Edwin Bliss	MacDonald	1983
Why Do I think I am Nothing without a Man	Penelope Russianoff	Bantam Books	1983
Bulimarexia	Marlene Bosking-White Phd, William C. White Jr PhD	George J. McLeod Ltd	1983
Body, Mind and Sugar	E.M. Abrahamson MD and A.W. Pezet	Holt Rinehart and Winston	1960
Sugar Blues	William Dufty	Abacus Press	1980
Taking the Rough with the Smooth	Dr Andrew Stanway	Pan Books Ltd	1981
Fit or Fat	Covert Bailey	Pelham Books Ltd	1980
A Woman in Her Own Right	Anne Dickson	Quartet Books Ltd	1982
Let's Eat Right to Keep Fit	Adelle Davis	Unwin Hyman Ltd	1984
Not All in the Mind	Dr Richard Mackarness	Pan Books Ltd	1982
Low Blood Sugar	Martin Budd	Thorsons	1981

The Premenstrual Syndrome	Caroline Shreeve	Thorsons	1983
Once a Month	Katharine Dalton	Fontana	1978
Release from Nervous Tension	D.H. Fink	Unwin Hyman Ltd	1984
The Superwoman Trap and How to Escape it	Cathy Douglas	Futura	1984
Addicts and Addictions	Dr Vernon Coleman	Corgi	1987
Addictions	Liz Hodgkinson	Thorsons	1986
Pure White and Deadly	John Yudkin	Davis-Poynter	1972
Making the Most of Yourself	Gill Cox and Sheila Dainow	Sheldon Press	1985